Dear Reader,

Like most people, I spend a lot of time watching my budget to make sure I am **spending my money wisely**. While I love to go out to eat, prices seem to keep going up and my budget does not stretch as far as it used to.

I find myself looking for ways to make my favorite restaurant dishes at home so I can indulge in all the restaurant meals I love while keeping my budget in mind. That is the inspiration for this book! From selections at sit-down dining restaurants like LongHorn Steakhouse, The Cheesecake Factory, and P.F. Chang's to items at more casual spots like Panera, Chipotle, and Chick-fil-A, this book has recipes that will **help you re-create** dishes you and your family love for a fraction of the price. You will find recipes for popular restaurant offerings from breakfast all the way to dessert, with the recipes arranged to cover every meal and occasion. There is also a Drinks chapter with recipes to re-create coffee shop classics as well as popular restaurant cocktails.

So if you are looking for **delicious recipes** that will satisfy your cravings and help you save a little money, all while having some fun in the kitchen, you are in the right place. Enjoy!

Kelly Jaggers

Welcome to the Everything® Series!

These handy, accessible books give you all you need to tackle a difficult project, gain a new hobby, comprehend a fascinating topic, prepare for an exam, or even brush up on something you learned back in school but have since forgotten.

You can choose to read an Everything® book from cover to cover or just pick out the information you want from our four useful boxes: Questions, Facts, Alerts, and Essentials. We give you everything you need to know on the subject, but throw in a lot of fun stuff along the way too.

question	fact
Answers to common questions.	Important snippets of information.

alert	essential
Urgent warnings.	Quick handy tips.

We now have more than 600 Everything® books in print, spanning such wide-ranging categories as cooking, health, parenting, personal finance, wedding planning, word puzzles, and so much more. When you're done reading them all, you can finally say you know Everything®!

PUBLISHER Karen Cooper

MANAGING EDITOR Lisa Laing

ASSOCIATE COPY DIRECTOR Casey Ebert

PRODUCTION EDITOR Jo-Anne Duhamel

ACQUISITIONS EDITOR Julia Belkas

DEVELOPMENT EDITOR Brett Palana-Shanahan

EVERYTHING® SERIES COVER DESIGNER Erin Alexander

THE
EVERYTHING®
RESTAURANT
COPYCAT
RECIPES
COOKBOOK

200 EASY RECIPES TO RE-CREATE YOUR FAVORITE RESTAURANT DISHES AT HOME

KELLY JAGGERS

ADAMS MEDIA

NEW YORK   AMSTERDAM/ANTWERP   LONDON   TORONTO   SYDNEY   NEW DELHI

This book is dedicated to you, dear reader.
I hope this book is one you turn to again and again. Happy cooking!

Acknowledgments

A book takes so much effort to go from idea to final product. I could not do this
without the excellent team at Adams Media to make it all happen. Thank you!
Special thanks go to Julia, Erin, Frank, and Lisa, who have worked
with me through the years and have helped me grow as an author and
a photographer. I appreciate you all more than you know.

Adams Media
An Imprint of Simon & Schuster, LLC
100 Technology Center Drive
Stoughton, Massachusetts 02072

Copyright © 2025 by Simon & Schuster, LLC.

All rights reserved, including the right to reproduce this book
or portions thereof in any form whatsoever. For information,
address Adams Media Subsidiary Rights Department,
1230 Avenue of the Americas, New York, NY 10020.

An Everything® Series Book.

Everything® and everything.com® are registered trademarks
of Simon & Schuster, LLC.

First Adams Media trade paperback edition March 2025

ADAMS MEDIA and colophon are registered trademarks of
Simon & Schuster, LLC.

For information about special discounts for bulk purchases,
please contact Simon & Schuster Special Sales at 1-866-506-
1949 or business@simonandschuster.com.

The Simon & Schuster Speakers Bureau can bring authors
to your live event. For more information or to book an event,
contact the Simon & Schuster Speakers Bureau at 1-866-
248-3049 or visit our website at www.simonspeakers.com.

Photographs by Kelly Jaggers

Manufactured in China

10 9 8 7 6 5 4 3 2 1

Library of Congress Cataloging-in-Publication Data has been
applied for.

ISBN 978-1-5072-2323-9
ISBN 978-1-5072-2324-6 (ebook)

This book is not authorized, approved, licensed, or endorsed
by the various restaurants that appear in this book. The recipes
in this book were not provided by the included restaurants
but are the author's creations based upon her most successful
efforts to replicate the various dishes. All rights to the various
restaurant and recipe names used in this book, which are
either registered or otherwise claimed as trademarks, are fully
reserved by the various corporations who own these rights.

Always follow safety and commonsense cooking protocols
while using kitchen utensils, operating ovens and stoves,
and handling uncooked food. If children are assisting in the
preparation of any recipe, they should always be supervised by
an adult.

Contains material adapted from the following title published
by Adams Media, an Imprint of Simon & Schuster, LLC:
The Everything® Restaurant Recipes Cookbook by Becky Bopp,
copyright © 2011, ISBN 978-1-4405-1125-7.

Contents

CHAPTER 6: BEEF, CHICKEN, AND PORK ENTRÉES 127

CHAPTER 10: DESSERTS   215

CHAPTER 11: DRINKS   243

Introduction

Everyone has a favorite restaurant meal that they crave, but going out to eat can be expensive. Luckily, you can make the same delicious dishes at home you would order at your favorite restaurants but for a fraction of the cost! With the two hundred copycat recipes in *The Everything® Restaurant Copycat Recipes Cookbook*, you can easily re-create the dining out experience at home—and each dish costs less per serving to make than it does to order at the restaurant!

The recipes in this book are arranged similar to a restaurant menu—by type of dish—so you can easily navigate to the section you need for any meal, occasion, or craving. The fun part of cooking restaurant recipes at home is that you can mix and match menu items from different places to customize a meal you and your family will really enjoy! Imagine a dinner made up of your favorite restaurant recipes: Spinach & Artichoke Dip from Applebee's for your appetizer, Parmesan Crusted Chicken from LongHorn Steakhouse for your main dish, and Cheddar Bay Biscuits from Red Lobster and Cilantro Lime Rice from Chipotle for your sides. Throw in a dessert of Ultimate Peanut Butter Cookies from Crumbl and you have a custom meal sure to please!

Cooking restaurant recipes at home has a number of benefits aside from cost savings. It allows you to customize recipes to suit your taste and dietary restrictions. Preparing these dishes at home also allows for easy customization for allergies. You can swap regular flour for gluten-free flour, swap meat and dairy for your favorite alternatives, and sub in allergy-friendly seed butters, condiments, and sauces. Cooking at home also allows for better portion control, so there will always be room for dessert!

The recipes in this book use ingredients that are easy to find at your local grocery store—and are prepared using common kitchen tools. You will also find tips and information in the first chapter to help you shop and cook with confidence, including information on food safety and stocking your pantry. With easy-to-follow steps, cooks of any level will feel happy with their finished dishes and get that restaurant experience at home.

The Everything® Restaurant Copycat Recipes Cookbook will be your guide for satisfying and fun meals all week long. Enjoy a satisfying breakfast from Cracker Barrel, lunch from Olive Garden, midday pick-me-up from Starbucks, and dinner from California Pizza Kitchen all while staying on budget! With recipe copycats this good, you may never dine out again!

CHAPTER 1

Creating the Restaurant Feeling at Home

If you and your family are among those who dine out often, you know that the cost adds up quickly. However, you will be amazed at the savings you will accumulate when you use a restaurant copycat recipe instead of dining out. Food prepared at home can be as delicious as food ordered at a five-star restaurant—and you don't have to be a master chef to cook these dishes either. All you need are a few simple tools. This chapter breaks down the equipment needed into appliances, cooking gadgets, cookware, and bakeware. You'll also learn the techniques required to make a wonderful restaurant-quality meal. With the tools in this book, you can make popular restaurant recipes your guests will swear were purchased from the restaurant that made the dish famous!

Appliances and Cookware

Cooking with the right tools makes mealtime easier, especially on busy days! This section outlines some handy tools, equipment, and appliances that can be helpful when preparing recipes in this book.

Appliances

These appliances are used throughout this book, and will make cooking easier and in many cases more flavorful:

- **Handheld electric mixer**—A portable handheld mixer will do well for the recipes in this book.
- **Blender**—This kitchen helper cuts time instantly by blending, chopping, and puréeing foods.
- **Deep fryer**—A small electric deep fryer will regulate the temperature of the cooking oil when deep-frying meats or vegetables to ensure even cooking. A skillet with deep sides and an oil and candy thermometer are a good substitute for a deep fryer.
- **Slow cooker**—A slow cooker is a great option when you want a home-cooked meal on busy days. Slow-cooked meals are generally very flavorful and require minimal labor from the cook once everything is added and the temperature is set.
- **Smokeless electric indoor grill**—This is a great tool to get grill flavor inside your kitchen. You can also use a cast iron grill pan if you do not have an electric grill.

- **Microwave oven**—Microwaves are excellent for quick thawing meat and vegetables and for reheating.

Cooking Tools

Good-quality knives that are well maintained can accomplish more in the kitchen than any electronic device. These are the knives you will need:

- A **chef's knife** that has a broad, tapered shape, which can easily be rocked over ingredients.
- A **bread knife**, which has a serrated edge that makes it perfect for cutting through crusts.
- A **paring knife**, which has a short blade for peeling, trimming, coring, and seeding vegetables.
- A **knife sharpener or steel**, which is used for sharpening the edge of a blade for easy cutting. It is a good idea to sharpen your knives once a week.

> **fact**
>
> Cooking in the kitchen can be fun, but it is important to keep safety in mind. Here are some basic safety rules you should follow to make your cooking experience safer and more enjoyable: Wear closed-toe shoes when you are working in the kitchen, especially when using knives; become familiar with your kitchen tools and how to use them safely; read the instruction manuals for your appliances.

Other Tools

Other tools needed include:

- Bottle opener
- Can opener
- Colander
- Cutting board
- Grater
- Long-handled forks, spoons, and spatulas
- Meat mallet
- Pizza cutter
- Rolling pin
- Set of measuring cups
- Set of measuring spoons
- Set of mixing bowls

Cookware

You'll also need these pieces of cookware:

- Saucepans with lids (1-quart, 2-quart, and 3-quart)
- 8-inch cast iron skillet
- 10-inch cast iron skillet
- 12-inch nonstick skillet
- 8-quart stockpot
- 5½-quart Dutch oven
- 2-burner nonstick griddle

Bakeware

Don't forget these necessary pieces of bakeware:

- Baking sheets (quarter size and half size)
- Baking dishes (8-inch × 8-inch and 9-inch × 13-inch)
- 12-cup muffin pan

- 24-cup mini muffin pan
- 9-inch and 10-inch pie pans
- 14-inch pizza pan
- 5-inch and 8-inch ramekins
- 16-inch roasting pan with a rack

Stocking the Pantry

Cooking is easier when you have a pantry stocked with the ingredients you need to prepare your favorite meals. Having a well-stocked pantry is a cook's secret weapon. Here is a list of basic ingredients that should be in your pantry. Of course, you can adjust items on the list to suit you and your family's likes and dislikes.

Herbs and Spices

While not comprehensive, this list of basic herbs and spices should be a good starting point for any well-stocked pantry:

- Chili powder
- Ground cinnamon
- Ground and whole cloves
- Ground nutmeg
- Dried basil
- Dried oregano
- Dried parsley
- Dried thyme
- Garlic powder
- Ground cumin
- Onion powder
- Paprika

If you've spent any time in the spice aisle at the supermarket, you know how expensive spices are. A convenient and cost-saving way to add extra flavor is to buy seasoning blends. Some of the most widely used flavors are:

- **Grill seasoning** contains a variety of pepper, salt, and spices that are good sprinkled onto meat before grilling, roasting, or broiling.
- **Cajun seasoning** is a blend of red pepper, garlic, onion, salt, and black pepper used to add a hot taste to any dish.
- **Italian seasoning** is a mix of basil, oregano, and other herbs and is useful in most pasta dishes.
- **Lemon pepper seasoning** adds flavor to poultry and vegetables.
- **Taco seasoning** contains a mixture of peppers, garlic, salt, and cumin suitable for tacos, fajitas, and enchiladas.

essential

A great way to stock your pantry with spices is to buy one or two new ones each time you go shopping and buy fresh herbs only when needed.

Sauces

Sauces are a great way to add flavor to your dishes. Here are some sauces you should have on hand in your kitchen:

- Barbecue sauce
- Chili sauce
- Condensed soups in a can (cream of mushroom and cream of chicken)
- Hot pepper sauce
- Olive oil
- Packages of dried onion soup mix
- Packages of ranch salad dressing mix and Italian salad dressing mix
- Soy sauce
- Steak sauce
- Teriyaki sauce
- Vinegar (red, rice, and balsamic)
- Wine (red and white suitable for drinking)
- Worcestershire sauce

Basic Grocery Items

You also need some essential grocery items, things you will find yourself using over and over in myriad recipes. These kitchen basics include:

- Beans (a variety of canned and dried)
- Bouillon cubes and powders
- Bread crumbs
- Cooking oil
- Croutons
- Graham crackers
- Meats (canned tuna, chicken, crab, and clams)
- Olives (black and green)
- Pastas (a variety)
- Rice (white, long grain, wild, and brown)
- Salsa
- Tomatoes (a variety of canned)
- Tomato sauce

Baking Items

To bake like the best restaurants, you need to keep some baking basics in your pantry, including:

- All-purpose flour
- Baking mix
- Baking powder
- Baking soda
- Brown sugar, light and dark
- Cocoa powder
- Confectioners' sugar
- Cornstarch
- Flavored chips (chocolate, peanut butter, and caramel)
- Granulated sugar
- Honey
- Nuts (a variety)
- Pancake mix
- Sweetened condensed milk
- Vegetable oil
- Yeast

Dessert Helpers

To create many restaurant-inspired desserts, you should have the following on hand:

- Cake mix
- Caramel sauce
- Pudding mix

Refrigerated Staples

Keep these items handy in the refrigerator so you can whip up your favorite copycat recipes without having to run out to the store. Make sure to have:

- Butter or margarine
- Cheeses (Cheddar, Monterey jack, Swiss, Parmesan, sliced American, etc.)
- Eggs, large
- Heavy cream
- Ketchup
- Mayonnaise
- Milk (whole)
- Mustard
- Sour cream

Frozen Goods

There are a few items that, while you won't use them every day, you'll still want to keep stocked in your freezer. They include:

- Boneless, skinless chicken breasts
- Bread and pizza dough
- Ground beef
- Steaks
- Vegetables (broccoli, spinach, and sliced green peppers)

With all these items on hand, you can put together a tasty and beautifully presented restaurant copycat meal in just a few minutes. The only thing you'll have to worry about is which recipe you want to try next.

Choosing Ingredients

Cooking from scratch always tastes better. Restaurant chefs seek out the freshest ingredients they can find and so should you. Skip the prepackaged items whenever you can. Generic brands may offer a lower price, but be careful to check out the quality and flavor—you may not be satisfied with the final taste of the dish. By upgrading your choices, you can turn an ordinary meal into something special. For example, instead of using plain iceberg lettuce, try romaine or a spring mix, and try using different types of cheeses like smoked or aged varieties. Experiment and try new flavors.

Meats

Red meats should have a fresh pink color and look moist. Meat packages should be firmly wrapped, with no leaking or excess moisture. Check expiration dates and package labeling to make sure that the meat is fresh and has been handled properly. Refrigerate meats as soon as they are purchased. Price is not always a reflection of quality; don't assume that the most expensive meat is the best.

CHICKEN

You can buy a chicken whole or in any variety of precut packages. Chicken should be plump and moist in the package. The key to cooking with chicken is to be careful to avoid cross contamination and the risk of salmonella. Wash your hands using warm water and soap before and after handling raw chicken. Keep uncooked chicken away from everything else on the kitchen counter. Use a separate cutting board and knife just for the uncooked chicken and do not use those same utensils for anything else. Thoroughly clean anything the chicken touches. If you follow these precautions, cooking with chicken is perfectly safe.

GROUND BEEF

According to the USDA, ground beef cannot contain more than 30 percent fat by weight, so all packages will state their fat content. Get to know your local butchers, and when a London broil or other roast goes on sale, have them grind it up for you to get premium ground beef at a reduced price.

STEAK AND ROAST

How do you tell a great steak from a regular steak? The things to look for when buying a steak are the grade and the cut. Grade refers to the age of the animal and the marbling of the meat. The USDA grades the best steaks as prime, followed by choice and select. When selecting a steak, always take a look at the marbling, or streaks of fat running through the meat. You want thin, evenly distributed streaks, which produce the best flavor. Cuts of steak are taken from different sections of the animal: The rib produces rib roast, back ribs, and rib eye steaks; the short loin produces the tastiest steaks like the T-bone, porterhouse, New York strip, and the best cut of tenderloin.

PORK

All pork found in retail stores is inspected by the USDA or by state systems with standards equal to the federal government's. When buying pork, look for cuts with a relatively small amount of fat and with meat that is firm and pink in color. For the best flavor, the meat should have a small amount of marbling. There are four basic cuts into which all other cuts are separated: the leg, side, loin, and shoulder. From those cuts, you get bacon, ground pork for sausage, ribs, roasts, chops, and ham.

FISH

Knowing how to choose fresh fish is a skill all cooks should have. A fresh whole fish should smell like clean water. The eyes of the fish should be bright and clear, and the gills should be a rich bright red. For fish fillets, look for fillets that are firm, not slimy or sticky, and have a mild, fresh smell. If any fish smells "fishy," looks discolored, or feels sticky or mushy, don't buy it.

Fruits

Look for tenderness, plumpness, and bright color when choosing your fruit. Fruits should be heavy for their size and free of bruises, cuts, mildew, mold, or any other blemishes.

- Bananas are sold in any stage of ripeness and should be stored at room temperature.
- Berries should separate easily from their stems. Wash berries when you bring them home, dry thoroughly, and store in a paper towel–lined container in the refrigerator.
- Melons that have a sweet aromatic scent should be chosen. A strong smell indicates that they are overripe. Always wash the outside of your melons before slicing.
- Oranges, grapefruits, and lemons are picked and sold when they are ripe. You may store them in the refrigerator for 2–3 weeks. Look for plump fruit with bright, shiny skin.

Vegetables

Take the time to inspect each vegetable before you buy. Look for crisp, plump, and brightly colored vegetables. Avoid the ones that are shriveled, bruised, moldy, or blemished.

- Asparagus should have straight stalks that are compact, with closed tips.

- Broccoli heads that are light green, have dark spots, or are yellowing should be avoided.
- Cabbage should be tight and have bright leaves with no brown spots.
- Cauliflower with withered leaves and brown spots should be bypassed.
- Celery stalks should have firm, crisp ribs.
- Cucumbers should be firm and not have soft spots.
- Green beans that are brightly colored and crisp are the best to select.
- Mushrooms are fresh when they are firm, plump, and without bruises.
- Peppers that are crisp and bright colored are the ones to choose.
- Spinach leaves should be crisp and free of moisture.
- Split peas that are shriveled or have brown spots should be avoided.

Cooking Terms and Techniques

Success in the kitchen starts with an understanding of cooking vocabulary, and good technique is the key to cooking a great restaurant-quality meal.

Most ingredients are cut into smaller pieces before being used in a recipe. Sometimes you want the pieces uniform in shape and size; other times it doesn't matter. Here are the basic cutting techniques:

- **Chopping** refers to simply cutting into smaller pieces. It results in a larger cut than a dice or a mince and the cuts don't have to be uniform. To chop vegetables, keep the tip of the chef's knife on the cutting board and cut down through the vegetable with a rocking motion. Feed the item being chopped toward the blade, keeping your fingers curled tight.
- **Dicing** results in a cube that is usually ¼-inch-square to ¾-inch-square. To dice something, cut it into sections as thick as you want your dice to be. Stack the sections and cut matchsticks in the uniform desired width. Then line up your matchsticks and cut them into a dice.
- **Mincing** is a very thin cut of food. To mince something, chop it roughly on a cutting board. Gather up the pieces in a pile. Position your knife above the pile. Keeping the tip touching the cutting board, repeatedly raise and lower the length of the blade down through whatever you're mincing, moving the blade in an arc.
- **Grating** gives food a very fine texture and can be done with a box grater or handheld grater.

- **Julienne** simply means to cut something into long strips. This is usually done with vegetables.
- **Slicing** is when you cut completely through an item such as meat, fruit, vegetables, cheese, or bread.
- **Zesting** is the process of removing the outer portion of a citrus fruit peel.

alert

A knife is an essential kitchen tool, which must be properly maintained in order to keep it in perfect working order. Knife maintenance is a necessary skill because a sharp knife is a safe knife. Take the time to sharpen your knives because a dull knife will slip and cause you to cut yourself.

There are various techniques for preparing meat and vegetables for cooking. Here are the basic terms you will need to know to make the recipes in this book:

- **"Al dente"** means "to the tooth" in Italian and is a term for pasta indicating that it is cooked just enough to maintain a firm texture.
- **Basting** involves moistening food during cooking with pan drippings or a sauce to prevent drying and add flavor.
- **Blanching** means to slightly cook food in boiling water.
- **Braising** is the recommended cooking method for tough cuts of meat, where they are cooked slowly in a small amount of liquid.
- **Brining** is to soak food in salted water.
- **Broil** means to cook food below direct heat.
- **Butterfly** means to split foods down the middle without completely separating the halves.
- **Deep-fry** is to cook food in enough hot oil to cover the food until crispy.
- **Marinate** means to soak food in a liquid in order to enhance the flavor of the food and tenderize it.
- **Poaching** involves cooking a food by submerging it in simmering liquid.
- **Roasting** is a method used to cook food in an oven.
- **Sauté** is to cook or brown food in a small amount of cooking oil.
- **Searing** involves browning meat quickly on high heat to seal in the juices.
- **Simmer** means to cook a food in liquid kept just below the boiling point.
- **Steaming** is the process of cooking food in the vapor given off by boiling water.
- **Stew** means to cook food in liquid in a covered pot for a long time until tender.
- **Stir-frying** is an Asian method of quickly cooking small pieces of food in hot oil while stirring constantly.

Food Presentation

Whenever you go to a restaurant, the atmosphere is almost as important as the quality of the food served in determining whether or not you have a fun and relaxing experience. Remember that food presentation and table setting are of utmost value when serving a restaurant copycat meal.

Garnishes

The ingredients in the dish can pull double duty as garnishes. Chop some extra-fresh herbs used in the dish to use as a garnish when plating. Diced tomatoes or thinly sliced green onion tops can add color and texture to a finished dish. A sprinkle of chopped fresh parsley is a quick way to add interest to your plate and can make a brown-colored dish appear more vibrant. Shredded or shaved cheeses add a nice touch to dishes like pasta, pizza, potatoes, and salad.

Plating

There are several types of plating techniques restaurants use, including:

- **Pie style** is where the plate is divided into a section each for the protein, starch, and vegetables.
- The **half-and-half style** of plating is where the main dish is on one side of the plate and the accompaniments on the other.
- **Vertical plating** is where you build the plate upward, usually with the protein on the bottom and the side dishes on top.
- **Family style plating** is where the food is served on large platters meant to be shared.

Presenting Desserts

To showcase your beautifully created restaurant desserts, think of ways to present them beautifully. Use small plates for dessert servings so they feel generous to the eye. For sliced desserts like cakes and pies, use a clean, sharp knife and wipe it off between cuts for cleaner slices. Most cakes can be jazzed up with a scoop of ice cream, and pie slices get a visual boost with a swirl of whipped cream and a sprig of fresh mint. Almost any dessert can be served with a few sliced berries on the side to add color and texture to the plate.

CHAPTER 2

Breakfast and Brunch

Bob Evans Sausage Gravy with Biscuits

This simple sausage gravy will give you all the flavors of a country breakfast and is served spooned over warm buttermilk biscuits. For a richer flavor, use half-and-half in place of milk.

1 pound roll pork sausage

¼ cup all-purpose flour

2 cups whole milk

½ teaspoon salt

½ teaspoon ground black pepper

8 Grands! Buttermilk Frozen Biscuits, prepared per package instructions

1 In a large skillet over medium heat, add sausage. Cook, crumbling well, until browned, about 8 minutes. Stir in flour and cook 1 minute. Gradually stir in milk, mixing until smooth.

2 Cook gravy until thick and bubbly, about 5–7 minutes, stirring constantly. Season with salt and pepper and stir well. Serve over hot biscuits.

Burger King French Toast Sticks

The secret to fluffy French toast sticks is to not let the batter soak into the bread too much, so dip each stick quickly and let excess batter drip off before shallow frying.

SERVES 4

4 slices Texas toast

2 large eggs, beaten

½ cup whole milk

2 tablespoons granulated sugar

1 tablespoon all-purpose flour

1 teaspoon pure vanilla extract

½ teaspoon ground cinnamon

½ cup vegetable oil

½ cup pancake syrup

1   Cut Texas toast slices into three strips each. Set aside.

2   In a blender, add eggs, milk, sugar, flour, vanilla, and cinnamon. Purée 20 seconds or until smooth. Transfer mixture to a medium bowl.

3   In a 10-inch cast iron skillet, add oil. Heat over medium-high heat until oil is hot, about 5 minutes.

4   Once oil is hot, dip Texas toast slices in batter until all sides are coated, but do not let bread become saturated. Let excess batter drip off 3–5 seconds, then add to skillet. Cook 1 minute per side or until golden brown and crisp. Transfer to a paper towel–lined plate to drain 20 seconds, then transfer to a serving plate. Serve hot, with syrup for dipping.

Burger King Fully Loaded Croissan'wich

SERVES 1

This breakfast sandwich is loaded with fluffy eggs, cheese, bacon, ham, and sausage. You can assemble it the night before and reheat it for 1 minute in the microwave.

2 ounces bulk breakfast sausage

2 strips thick-cut smoked bacon

1 large egg, beaten

2 (1-ounce) slices thin-sliced Black Forest ham

1 (1.5-ounce) all-butter croissant, sliced in half lengthwise

2 slices American cheese

1 Shape sausage into a thin patty and refrigerate 15 minutes.

2 Heat a 12-inch nonstick skillet over medium heat. Once hot, add bacon and cook, turning often, until bacon is crisp, about 13–15 minutes. Once crisp, transfer to a paper towel–lined plate and set aside. Pour off all but 1 tablespoon bacon fat and return skillet to medium heat.

3 To same skillet, add sausage patty and cook 2 minutes or until golden brown, then flip and cook 2–3 minutes more until sausage is fully cooked and golden on both sides. Transfer from pan to same plate with bacon and set aside.

4 To same skillet over medium heat, add egg. Immediately reduce heat to low and let bottom of egg set, about 15 seconds. Use a silicone or heatproof spatula to gently push edges of egg to center of pan while tilting pan so uncooked egg moves to edges until no wet egg remains, about 30 seconds. Flip egg and cook 20 seconds more, then transfer to plate with sausage.

5 Increase heat to medium and add ham to skillet. Cook 20 seconds per side or until ham is hot. Transfer to plate with sausage.

6 To same skillet, add croissant cut side down. Cook 45 seconds or until cut side is just starting to toast. Transfer to plate cut side up.

7 Place egg on bottom half of croissant. Top with sausage patty, 1 slice American cheese, ham slices, bacon, remaining slice American cheese, and top half of croissant. Serve immediately.

Cinnabon Cinnamon Rolls

Cinnabon was founded in 1985 and is famous for their soft and gooey cinnamon rolls. This version is easy to make since the recipe uses prepared pizza dough. It is sure to become a family favorite.

SERVES 12

1 (13.8-ounce) tube refrigerated pizza dough

1 cup packed light brown sugar

2½ tablespoons ground cinnamon

⅓ cup plus 4 tablespoons softened unsalted butter, divided

3 ounces cream cheese

1½ cups confectioners' sugar

½ teaspoon pure vanilla extract

⅛ teaspoon salt

1 Preheat oven to 400°F and lightly grease a 9-inch × 13-inch baking dish.

2 Spread pizza dough on a lightly floured surface.

3 Combine brown sugar and cinnamon in a small bowl. Set aside.

4 Spread ⅓ cup butter evenly over dough. Sprinkle brown sugar mixture evenly over surface of dough. Roll up long side of dough like a jelly roll.

5 Cut dough into twelve even slices and place in prepared baking dish cut side up. Bake rolls 15 minutes or until golden brown.

6 While rolls are baking, combine remaining butter, cream cheese, confectioners' sugar, vanilla, and salt in a medium bowl. Blend well with an electric mixer until fluffy, about 3 minutes. Spread icing over warm rolls. Serve.

CINNABON CINNAMON ROLLS

Cracker Barrel Fried Apples

These fried apples are a popular breakfast side dish at Cracker Barrel. They are also great with pork chops or served on top of pancakes or ice cream.

SERVES 8

8 medium red apples, unpeeled

¼ pound unsalted butter

½ cup granulated sugar

1 teaspoon ground cinnamon

⅛ teaspoon ground nutmeg

1 Slice apples into about ½-inch-thick slices.

2 In a 12-inch nonstick skillet over medium heat, add butter. Once melted, add apples and sugar to skillet. Place lid on skillet and cook 20 minutes or until apples are tender and juicy.

3 Sprinkle with cinnamon and nutmeg before serving.

Cracker Barrel Hashbrown Casserole

SERVES 6

THE CRACKER BARREL OLD COUNTRY STORE

The Cracker Barrel restaurant chain has a Southern-themed country store at each location with rocking chairs on the front porch. The menu consists of Southern comfort food, and breakfast is served all day.

This is a wonderful breakfast side dish at Cracker Barrel that can be enjoyed any time of day. You can make it up to three days ahead of time and put it in the oven for an hour before you plan to eat it for an easy side or meal.

1 pound frozen hashbrowns

¼ cup salted butter, melted

1 (10-ounce) can cream of chicken soup

½ pint full-fat sour cream

¼ cup chopped yellow onion

1 cup grated medium Cheddar cheese

½ teaspoon salt

⅛ teaspoon ground black pepper

1 Preheat oven to 350°F.

2 Spray a large baking dish with nonstick cooking spray.

3 In a large bowl, combine all ingredients. Transfer to baking dish and spread evenly in dish.

4 Bake 45 minutes or until browned on top. Serve.

Cracker Barrel Momma's French Toast

The secret to Cracker Barrel's crave-worthy French toast is to use sourdough sandwich bread. It adds a savory tang that will keep you coming back for more!

SERVES 4

5 large eggs, beaten

½ cup whole milk

2 tablespoons all-purpose flour

2 tablespoons packed light brown sugar

2 teaspoons pure vanilla extract

¼ teaspoon salt

2 tablespoons unsalted butter, divided

8 slices sourdough sandwich bread

½ cup pancake syrup

1 In a medium bowl, add eggs, milk, flour, brown sugar, vanilla, and salt. Whisk well to combine.

2 Heat a 12-inch nonstick skillet over medium heat. Once hot, add 1 tablespoon butter.

3 Add a wire rack to a half sheet pan. Dip 4 slices bread in egg mixture, flipping bread to coat. Transfer bread to skillet and cook 2 minutes per side or until both sides are golden brown. Transfer toast slices to wire rack and repeat with remaining butter, bread, and egg mixture.

4 Cut French toast slices into triangles. Place four triangles on each serving plate. Serve immediately with syrup on the side.

Denny's Country Fried Steaks and Country Gravy

SERVES 4

Denny's serves these golden fried chopped beefsteaks smothered in rich country gravy. To replicate how Denny's serves them, pair with eggs, breakfast potatoes, and biscuits for a full meal!

Fried Steaks

1 cup all-purpose flour

1 teaspoon salt

½ teaspoon paprika

½ teaspoon ground black pepper

½ cup low-fat buttermilk

1 pound beef cube steak, cut into 4 pieces

¼ cup vegetable oil

Gravy

2 tablespoons vegetable oil

2 tablespoons all-purpose flour

2½ cups whole milk

¼ teaspoon salt

½ teaspoon ground black pepper

1 For the fried steak: In a shallow dish, stir together flour, salt, paprika, and pepper.
2 Place buttermilk in a separate shallow dish.
3 Dredge steaks in flour mixture, dip in buttermilk, and dip again in flour mixture.
4 Heat oil in a large skillet over medium-high heat.
5 Once hot, add steaks and cook 5 minutes on each side or until steaks are deep golden brown. Transfer steaks to a paper towel–lined plate to drain. Pour off any excess oil.
6 For the gravy: In same pan, heat oil over medium-high heat and whisk in flour. Stir constantly 5 minutes or until light brown in color.
7 Whisk in milk a little at a time until mixture thickens, about 5 minutes. Add salt and pepper and stir.
8 Serve steaks with gravy poured over top.

Denny's Pancake Puppies

Denny's has created many varieties of their Pancake Puppies through the years, including cinnamon sugar, strawberry, chocolate, and red velvet. This recipe is a copycat of the classic version studded with sweet blueberries.

SERVES 1
(YIELDS 6 PANCAKE BALLS)

Vegetable oil, for frying, plus more for coating ice cream scoop

1 cup pancake mix

⅓ cup whole milk

1 large egg

½ cup chopped dried blueberries

1 tablespoon finely chopped white chocolate chips

Confectioners' sugar, for dusting

1 Fill deep fryer with oil per manufacturer directions and heat to 350°F, or in a 5½-quart Dutch oven add enough oil to fill pot by 3 inches, leaving at least 3 inches of space at the top, and place over medium-high heat until oil reaches 350°F.

2 In a medium bowl, combine pancake mix, milk, and egg. Add blueberries and chocolate chips and stir. Let batter sit 10 minutes to thicken.

3 Use an ice cream scoop coated with oil to make a batter ball and drop batter ball in hot oil. Cook 2½–3 minutes until dark brown.

4 Remove from pan and drain on paper towels. Dust with confectioners' sugar and repeat with remaining batter. Serve hot.

Denny's Santa Fe Skillet

SERVES 1

WHAT'S IN A NAME?

Denny's was founded in 1953 in Lakewood, California, as Danny's Donuts, and the restaurant's original concept was coffee and doughnuts. In 1956 they rebranded to Danny's Coffee Shops, then in 1959 to Denny's Coffee Shops to avoid customer confusion with another restaurant, Coffee Dan's. In 1961 they dropped the "coffee shops" and became simply "Denny's."

Skillets have been on the menu at Denny's since 2008, and the Santa Fe Skillet has been a customer favorite. While the eggs here are prepared sunny-side up, feel free to make them your favorite way.

2 tablespoons vegetable oil

1 cup diced red skin potatoes

2 teaspoons Lawry's Seasoned Salt

¼ cup water

1 tablespoon unsalted butter

2 large eggs

¼ cup crumbled chorizo sausage

½ cup sliced button mushrooms

¼ cup frozen fire-roasted onions and peppers

½ cup shredded medium Cheddar cheese

1 Heat oil in a medium cast iron skillet over medium heat. Add potatoes to pan and sprinkle with seasoned salt. Add water, cover skillet with a lid, and cook 5 minutes. Remove lid and continue to cook, stirring occasionally, 10–12 minutes until potatoes are golden brown and tender. Transfer to a plate and set aside.

2 To same skillet over medium heat, add butter. Once butter is melted and foaming, add eggs. Cook 3–4 minutes until whites are set but yolks are still soft. Transfer to a plate and set aside.

3 To same skillet over medium heat, add chorizo and mushrooms and cook 5–6 minutes until chorizo is cooked through and mushrooms are tender.

4 Drain off excess fat from skillet and stir in cooked potatoes and fire-roasted onions and peppers. Cook 3–4 minutes more until all vegetables are tender.

5 Remove skillet from heat and sprinkle with cheese. Top with prepared eggs. Serve hot.

IHOP Chicken Fajita Omelette

Fajitas are not just for sizzling platters, quesadillas, and nachos. At IHOP they are also for breakfast! If you have leftover chicken fajita filling from dinner earlier in the week, this is an excellent way to use it.

2 large eggs

1 teaspoon water

½ cup leftover chicken fajita filling (chicken, onions, and peppers)

½ cup shredded Mexican cheese blend

¼ cup salsa

1 In a small bowl, beat together eggs and water.

2 Heat a 10-inch skillet over medium heat. Add egg mixture and cook 1 minute, then using a spatula, draw edges of eggs into center and tilt pan to let uncooked eggs run to edges of pan. Continue until eggs are set.

3 Add chicken, onions, and peppers. Fold omelette in half. Turn off heat. Top omelette with cheese and salsa.

4 Cover skillet with a lid and let sit 2 minutes or until cheese melts. Serve immediately.

IHOP Colorado Omelette

SERVES 2

Although IHOP is famous for its pancakes, waffles, and crepes, they offer a variety of egg dishes including eight different types of omelettes—even a build-your-own option. The Colorado is the best omelette for meat lovers. Serve garnished with green onions and salsa.

2 tablespoons salted butter

¼ cup diced yellow onion

¼ cup diced green pepper

⅛ cup water

4 large eggs

¼ teaspoon salt

¼ cup diced tomatoes

¼ cup cooked and diced bacon

¼ cup cooked and diced ham

¼ cup cooked and sliced breakfast sausage links

¼ cup diced deli roast beef

¾ cup shredded medium Cheddar cheese, divided

1 In a 10-inch skillet over medium heat, add butter. Once butter is melted, add onion and pepper to skillet. Sauté until tender, about 5 minutes. Remove from skillet and reserve.

2 In a medium mixing bowl, add water, eggs, and salt. Stir and beat well.

3 Return skillet to medium heat. Add egg mixture and cook 1 minute, then using a spatula, draw edges of eggs into center and tilt pan to let uncooked eggs run to edges of pan. Continue until eggs are set.

4 Add cooked onions and pepper, tomatoes, and all meats plus ½ cup cheese. Fold omelette in half and top with remaining cheese. Serve immediately.

IHOP New York Cheesecake Pancakes

New York Cheesecake Pancakes have become one of IHOP's most popular signature pancakes. They feature rich cream cheese-studded pancakes topped with strawberry jam and whipped cream.

**SERVES 5
(YIELDS 15 PANCAKES)**

1 (8-ounce) package cream cheese

2 cups pancake mix

½ cup graham cracker crumbs

¼ cup granulated sugar

1 cup whole milk

2 large eggs

1 Slice cream cheese into four pieces and freeze overnight.

2 The next day, preheat a griddle over medium-high heat.

3 In a large bowl, combine pancake mix, graham cracker crumbs, sugar, milk, and eggs. Cut frozen cream cheese into bite-sized pieces and add to batter.

4 Spray griddle with nonstick cooking spray.

5 Add ⅓ cup batter onto hot griddle and cook 2 minutes per side or until browned. Transfer to a plate and cover with a clean towel to keep warm while you prepare remaining batter. Repeat with remaining batter. Serve.

IHOP Original Buttermilk Pancakes

**SERVES 4
(YIELDS 8 PANCAKES)**

IHOP is best known for their stacks of fluffy buttermilk pancakes. They are usually served with butter and pancake syrup, but IHOP also has a variety of flavored syrups at the table including blueberry, strawberry, and butter pecan. Choose your favorite syrup to serve with these delicious pancakes.

1⅓ cups all-purpose flour

1 teaspoon baking powder

1 teaspoon baking soda

½ teaspoon salt

1⅓ cups low-fat buttermilk

1 large egg

¼ cup vegetable oil

¼ cup granulated sugar

1 In a medium bowl, combine flour, baking powder, baking soda, and salt. Whisk to combine.

2 In a separate medium bowl, combine buttermilk, egg, oil, and sugar and whisk until smooth.

3 Add wet ingredients to dry ingredients and mix with a spatula until just combined and no large clumps of flour remain, about 20 strokes.

4 Preheat a 2-burner griddle over medium heat and spray with nonstick cooking spray.

5 Add two ⅓ cup scoops of batter onto hot griddle and cook 2–4 minutes per side until browned. Transfer to a plate and cover with a clean towel to keep warm while you prepare remaining batter. Serve warm.

IHOP ORIGINAL BUTTERMILK PANCAKES

MCDONALD'S BACON, EGG & CHEESE BISCUIT

McDonald's Bacon, Egg & Cheese Biscuit

Frozen buttermilk biscuits make this breakfast sandwich easy to prepare any day of the week and also make this recipe easy to double, triple, or more.

SERVES 1

1 Grands! Frozen Buttermilk Biscuit, prepared per package instructions

1 teaspoon salted butter, melted

1 slice thick-cut smoked bacon

1 large egg

2 tablespoons water

1 slice American cheese

1 When biscuit comes out of oven, brush it with melted butter. Slice in half lengthwise and set aside to cool.

2 Heat a 12-inch nonstick skillet over medium heat. Once hot, add bacon. Cook, turning often, until crisp, about 12–15 minutes. Transfer to a paper towel–lined plate to drain.

3 Drain all but 1 teaspoon bacon fat from skillet and reduce heat to low. In a small bowl add egg and water and beat with a fork until fluffy, about 30 seconds. Add egg to pan and swirl to coat pan evenly. Let stand 30–45 seconds or until just set. Carefully flip and let cook 30–45 seconds more or until egg is cooked through. Remove egg to a cutting board and fold in half, then fold sides into center to form a square.

4 To assemble, place cheese on bottom of biscuit. Break bacon slice in half and place on cheese. Top with folded egg and top biscuit. Serve immediately.

McDonald's Breakfast Burritos

THE FIRST FAST-FOOD BREAKFAST

McDonald's pioneered the breakfast fast-food concept with the introduction of the Egg McMuffin in 1972. The sandwich was created by franchise owner Herb Petersen, and the name was coined by Patty Turner, the wife of a corporate executive.

Nelly Quijano, a Cuban immigrant and McDonald's franchise owner from Houston, Texas, is credited with creating the chain's popular Breakfast Burrito. It was so popular it rolled out nationwide in 1989!

4 ounces bulk pork breakfast sausage

4 teaspoons minced yellow onion

½ tablespoon minced mild green chilies

4 large eggs, beaten

⅛ teaspoon salt

⅛ teaspoon ground black pepper

4 (8-inch) flour tortillas

4 slices American cheese

1 Preheat a medium skillet over medium heat. Add sausage and onion and sauté 3–4 minutes until sausage is browned. Add chilies and sauté 1 minute more.

2 Pour eggs into pan and scramble with sausage, onion, and chilies. Stir in salt and pepper.

3 Heat tortillas in microwave on a moist paper towel 1 minute.

4 Add a fourth of the egg mixture and 1 slice cheese to each tortilla and roll into a burrito. Serve.

Starbucks Bacon & Gruyère Egg Bites

Introduced in 2017, Starbucks Egg Bites were created for customers who ordered breakfast sandwiches without the bread. You can reheat leftovers in your microwave for 1 minute on 50 percent power.

SERVES 6
(YIELDS 12 EGG BITES)

8 large eggs

1 cup 4 percent milkfat cottage cheese

2 teaspoons cornstarch

¼ teaspoon ground black pepper

1 cup shredded Gruyère cheese

3 strips thick-cut bacon, cooked crisp and chopped

1. Preheat oven to 325°F. Lightly spray a 12-cup silicone muffin pan with nonstick cooking spray. Place muffin pan into a large roasting pan. Set aside.
2. Boil a kettle of water, then set aside.
3. In a blender, add eggs, cottage cheese, cornstarch, and pepper. Purée until smooth, about 1 minute.
4. Divide Gruyère cheese and bacon evenly between prepared muffin cups. Pour egg mixture evenly over top. Pour recently boiled water into roasting pan until it reaches halfway up muffin pan. Bake 25–30 minutes until egg bites are set in center.
5. Remove from oven and cool 30 minutes before removing muffin pan from roasting pan and removing egg bites from pan. Serve warm.

Waffle House Biscuits & Gravy

SERVES 2

Biscuits and gravy make a hearty, comfort food meal that will keep you full all morning long. Enjoy these alone or as a side with eggs and your favorite breakfast meat.

1 tablespoon unsalted butter

2 Grands! Frozen Buttermilk Biscuits, prepared per package instructions, sliced in half lengthwise

2 ounces bulk breakfast sausage

2 tablespoons vegetable oil

2 tablespoons all-purpose flour

2 cups whole milk

½ teaspoon ground black pepper

¼ teaspoon salt

1 In a 12-inch nonstick skillet over medium heat, add butter. Once butter is melted and foaming, add biscuits cut side down. Cook 2–3 minutes until cut sides of biscuits are golden brown. Transfer to serving plates.

2 To same skillet over medium heat, add sausage. Cook, crumbling well, until fully cooked and brown, about 5 minutes. Add oil and flour and cook, stirring constantly, 2 minutes.

3 Reduce heat to low and slowly stir in milk. Once all milk is added and mixture has no lumps of flour remaining, increase heat to medium and cook, stirring constantly, until gravy is thick, about 5–7 minutes.

4 Remove skillet from heat and stir in pepper and salt. Spoon gravy over prepared biscuits. Serve immediately.

Waffle House Cheesesteak Omelet

Waffle House omelets are prepared using a milkshake mixer to make them extra fluffy and smooth. To re-create this omelet at home, you can use a blender to make the eggs fluffy.

SERVES 1

1 portion frozen thin-sliced beefsteak, such as Steak-umm

3 large eggs

¼ teaspoon salt

2 tablespoons unsalted butter

2 slices American cheese

1 In an 8-inch nonstick skillet over medium heat, add beefsteak. Cook 1 minute, then break up beef with spatula and cook 1 minute more. Transfer to a paper towel–lined plate and set aside.

2 Add eggs and salt to a blender and purée 1 minute.

3 While eggs purée, add butter to same skillet over medium heat and once melted and foaming, swirl to coat pan. Add eggs to pan, constantly swirling pan, until bottoms are set and eggs are starting to puff.

4 Carefully flip omelet and cook 30 seconds, then flip again and add cooked beef and cheese slices. Reduce heat to low, fold omelet in half, and cook 15 seconds. Flip and cook 15–20 seconds more until cheese is melted. Transfer to a plate and serve immediately.

Waffle House Ham, Egg & Cheese Hashbrown Bowl

This hearty breakfast starts with a base of Waffle House Hash-browns that is topped with cheese, scrambled eggs, and ham. You can also use crumbled cooked sausage or chopped cooked bacon.

2 recipes Waffle House Hashbrowns, prepared (see recipe in this chapter)

2 slices American cheese

1 tablespoon unsalted butter

2 large eggs, beaten

½ cup diced ham

1 In a serving bowl, add hashbrowns and top with cheese slices. Set aside.

2 In an 8-inch skillet over medium heat, add butter. Once melted, swirl to coat bottom of pan and add eggs. Reduce heat to low and let eggs cook 20 seconds, then use a spatula to start scrambling eggs. Cook until eggs are set, about 1 minute. Transfer eggs to serving bowl.

3 Return skillet to medium heat and add ham. Cook, stirring often, until ham is hot and starting to brown, about 3 minutes. Transfer ham to bowl on top of eggs. Serve immediately.

Waffle House Hashbrowns

Whether you prefer them plain, with a drizzle of ketchup, or with a bit of salt and pepper, Waffle House Hashbrowns are by far the most popular side dish on the menu.

2 tablespoons salted butter

1 cup frozen shredded hashbrown potatoes

1 In a 12-inch nonstick skillet over medium heat, add butter. Once melted, swirl to coat bottom of pan and add hashbrowns in an even layer. Cover pan with a lid and cook 5 minutes, then remove lid and cook 2–3 minutes more until hashbrowns are golden brown.

2 Flip hashbrowns and press down gently with spatula. Continue to cook 5–7 minutes until second side is golden brown. Transfer to a plate and serve immediately.

SERVES 1

WAFFLE HOUSE HASHBROWN VARIATIONS

In 1984, Waffle House introduced a new hashbrown menu that allowed customers to customize their golden brown breakfast potatoes. Variations include smothered (topped with chopped onions when hashbrowns hit the griddle), covered (topped with a slice of American cheese after flipping), or chunked (topped with diced ham when hashbrowns hit the griddle).

Waffle House Waffles

SERVES 4

Waffle House Waffles are fluffy and tender, with a touch of vanilla. Letting the batter chill overnight helps make a fluffier waffle, but an hour will do in a pinch. Dress these up with butter and syrup fresh off the waffle iron.

1½ cups all-purpose flour

2 tablespoons cornstarch

¼ cup granulated sugar

½ teaspoon baking soda

½ teaspoon baking powder

¼ teaspoon salt

1 cup half-and-half

½ cup low-fat buttermilk

¼ cup unsalted butter, melted and cooled

1 large egg

1 teaspoon pure vanilla extract

1 In a medium bowl, add flour, cornstarch, sugar, baking soda, baking powder, and salt. Whisk well to combine. Set aside.

2 In another medium bowl, combine half-and-half, buttermilk, butter, egg, and vanilla. Whisk until thoroughly combined. Mix wet ingredients into dry ingredients until just combined with small lumps of flour remaining. Cover and chill at least 1 hour or overnight. Remove from refrigerator 20 minutes before you are ready to cook.

3 Preheat a waffle iron. Once hot, spray lightly with nonstick cooking spray. Add ½ cup waffle batter to center of iron, close, and bake 4–6 minutes until waffle is golden brown and crisp. Repeat with remaining batter.

4 Serve warm.

CHAPTER 3
Appetizers and Snacks

Applebee's Spinach & Artichoke Dip

SERVES 2

Anyone who has ever visited an Applebee's restaurant falls in love with their mouthwatering spinach and artichoke dip. Serve it with fresh bread or warm tortilla chips.

1 (14-ounce) can artichoke hearts, drained and chopped

1 (10-ounce) box frozen chopped spinach

1 (10-ounce) jar Alfredo sauce

1 cup shredded Parmesan and Romano cheese blend

2 medium Roma tomatoes, diced

4 ounces softened cream cheese

½ cup shredded mozzarella cheese

1 teaspoon minced fresh garlic

1 Combine all ingredients in a medium mixing bowl. Spread mixture evenly in a small baking dish.

2 Bake in a 350°F oven 30 minutes or until cheeses melt. Serve warm.

Auntie Anne's Pretzels

You can create this popular mall food at home. Auntie Anne's began as a stand at a farmers' market in 1988 and today has more than 1,200 locations including 600 international franchises.

SERVES 12

$3\frac{1}{2}$ cups warm water, divided

$1\frac{1}{8}$ teaspoons active dry yeast

2 tablespoons packed light brown sugar

$1\frac{1}{8}$ teaspoons salt

1 cup bread flour

3 cups all-purpose flour

2 tablespoons baking soda

3 tablespoons pretzel salt

4 tablespoons melted salted butter

1 Preheat oven to 400°F.

2 Add $1\frac{1}{2}$ cups water to a medium mixing bowl and add yeast. Stir to dissolve. Let stand 5 minutes.

3 To yeast mixture, add brown sugar and salt. Stir to dissolve. Add flours and knead dough by hand until smooth and elastic, about 12 minutes.

4 Let dough rise on the countertop at least 30 minutes or until doubled in bulk.

5 While dough is rising, combine remaining water and baking soda in a medium bowl. Stir often.

6 After dough has risen, divide into twelve pieces. Roll each piece into a 14-inch rope (about ½-inch or less thick) and lay rope on a work surface. Loop the rope in half and then twist the ends together two or three times. Pull the ends back over the loop to create the classic pretzel shape, pressing the ends into the pretzel to secure them.

7 Dip each pretzel in baking soda solution and place on a greased half baking sheet. Sprinkle with pretzel salt.

8 Bake 10 minutes or until golden. Brush with melted butter and serve.

Buffalo Wild Wings Asian Zing Cauliflower Wings

SERVES 4

Cauliflower wings are a popular alternative to chicken for vegetarians and those looking for a fun way to add more vegetables to their diet. This blend of crisp cauliflower and tangy sweet sauce is a fan favorite!

½ cup Thai sweet chili sauce

1 teaspoon light soy sauce

1 teaspoon lemon juice

1 teaspoon rice vinegar

⅛ teaspoon ground ginger

Vegetable oil, for frying

1 cup all-purpose flour

2 tablespoons cornstarch

½ teaspoon salt

½ teaspoon ground black pepper

¼ teaspoon onion powder

¼ teaspoon garlic powder

¼ teaspoon paprika

1 large egg

1 cup low-fat buttermilk

1 (2-pound) head cauliflower, cut into bite-sized florets

1 In a small bowl, combine Thai sweet chili sauce, soy sauce, lemon juice, vinegar, and ginger. Whisk well and set aside.

2 Fill deep fryer with oil per manufacturer directions and heat to 350°F, or in a 5½-quart Dutch oven add enough oil to fill pot by 3 inches, leaving at least 3 inches of space at the top, and place over medium-high heat until oil reaches 350°F.

3 In a large resealable plastic bag, add flour, cornstarch, salt, pepper, onion powder, garlic powder, and paprika. Close bag and shake well to combine. Set aside.

4 In a medium bowl, add egg and beat well. Add buttermilk and whisk to combine.

5 Add cauliflower florets to bag with flour, close, and shake to coat. Transfer florets to a plate. Dip florets in buttermilk mixture and then return to bag and coat in flour. Place florets on a wire rack while oil heats.

6 Fry 5 or 6 florets 5–6 minutes in hot oil, turning halfway through cooking time, until florets are golden brown and tender when pierced with a paring knife.

7 Transfer florets to a paper towel–lined plate to drain. Repeat with remaining cauliflower.

8 Once cauliflower is fried, add to a large bowl along with prepared sauce and toss to coat evenly. Serve immediately.

Buffalo Wild Wings Boneless Wings

Boneless wings at Buffalo Wild Wings are made from chunks of breaded chicken breast meat that are deep-fried and tossed in a buffalo wing sauce. They are a popular alternative to bone-in wings.

SERVES 4

1 cup all-purpose flour

2 tablespoons cornstarch

½ teaspoon salt

½ teaspoon ground black pepper

1 large egg

1 cup low-fat buttermilk

1 pound chicken breast tenders, cut into 1-inch pieces

Vegetable oil, for frying

½ cup buffalo wing sauce

1 In a large resealable plastic bag, add flour, cornstarch, salt, and pepper. Close bag and shake well to combine. Set aside.

2 In a medium bowl, add egg and beat well. Add buttermilk and whisk to combine.

3 Add chicken pieces to bag with flour, close, and shake to coat. Remove chicken pieces and place on a plate. Dip in buttermilk mixture and then return to bag and coat in flour. Place on a wire rack to let breading set while oil heats.

4 Fill deep fryer with oil per manufacturer directions and heat to 350°F, or in a 5½-quart Dutch oven add enough oil to fill pot by 3 inches, leaving at least 3 inches of space at the top, and place over medium-high heat until oil reaches 350°F.

5 Add 5 or 6 chicken pieces at a time to hot oil and cook 5–6 minutes, turning halfway through cooking time, until chicken is golden brown and reaches an internal temperature of 165°F.

6 Transfer chicken pieces to a paper towel–lined plate to drain. Repeat process with remaining chicken.

7 Once chicken is fried, add to a large bowl along with wing sauce and toss to coat evenly. Serve immediately.

Buffalo Wild Wings Cheddar Cheese Curds

SERVES 4

Buffalo Wild Wings serves these crispy cheese curds with a side of Southwest ranch dressing for dipping. They even add the crispy curds to their Cheese Curd Bacon Burger!

Vegetable oil, for frying

1¼ cups all-purpose flour, divided

1 teaspoon baking powder

¼ teaspoon salt

½ cup low-fat buttermilk

½ cup club soda

16 ounces Cheddar cheese curds, refrigerated

1 Fill deep fryer with oil per manufacturer directions and heat to 350°F, or in a 5½-quart Dutch oven add enough oil to fill pot by 3 inches, leaving at least 3 inches of space at the top, and place over medium-high heat until oil reaches 350°F.

2 In a medium bowl, combine 1 cup flour, baking powder, and salt. Whisk to combine, then add buttermilk and club soda and whisk until batter is smooth.

3 In a large resealable plastic bag, combine remaining flour with cheese curds. Seal bag and shake to evenly coat cheese curds. Remove from bag and tap off excess.

4 Working with 5 or 6 curds at a time, dip curds in batter 1 at a time and immediately add to hot oil. Fry 2 minutes per side or until puffed and golden brown.

5 Transfer cooked curds to a paper towel–lined plate to drain. Repeat with remaining curds. Serve immediately.

Buffalo Wild Wings Traditional Wings

Buffalo Wild Wings restaurants have a choice of twenty-six sauces and dry rubs for their wings. This recipe calls for traditional buffalo sauce, but feel free to mix it up. You can dress these wings in any wing sauce you love best and serve them with ranch or blue cheese dressing for dipping.

1 pound chicken wing pieces, flats and drumettes

1 teaspoon salt

Vegetable oil, for frying

½ cup buffalo wing sauce

1 Lay wings on a wire rack over a half sheet pan. Sprinkle both sides with salt. Refrigerate, uncovered, at least 4 hours or overnight.

2 Remove wings from refrigerator 30 minutes before frying to allow them to warm to room temperature.

3 Fill deep fryer with oil per manufacturer directions and heat to 350°F, or in a 5½-quart Dutch oven add enough oil to fill pot by 3 inches, leaving at least 3 inches of space at the top, and place over medium-high heat until oil reaches 350°F.

4 Fry wings in hot oil in batches 4–5 minutes until wings are golden brown and reach an internal temperature of 165°F. Transfer cooked wings to a paper towel–lined plate and repeat with remaining wings.

5 Place wings in a large bowl and add sauce. Toss to coat wings in sauce and then serve.

SERVES 4

BUFFALO WILD WINGS SAUCES

Store-bought wing sauce is very tasty, but did you know you can purchase authentic Buffalo Wild Wings sauces and rubs to use at home? They sell a range of their signature wing sauces and dry rubs in grocery stores, online, and in their restaurants.

The Cheesecake Factory Crispy Crab Bites

SERVES 6

These delicious little crab cakes are easy to prepare and will be a hit with family and guests. They make a great party snack or appetizer.

½ pound lump crabmeat

3 tablespoons plain bread crumbs

2 tablespoons mayonnaise

2 tablespoons minced green onions

2 tablespoons minced red bell peppers

½ large egg, beaten

1 teaspoon minced fresh parsley

1 teaspoon Old Bay Seasoning

½ teaspoon prepared yellow mustard

1 cup vegetable oil

¼ cup panko bread crumbs

1 In a large bowl, add all ingredients except oil and panko. Carefully fold ingredients together. Be sure not to overwork or lumps of crab will fall apart.

2 Using your hands or a spoon, fill 12 cups of an ungreased mini muffin pan with equal amounts of crab mixture. Press down gently on each so tops are flat. Don't press too hard or crab cakes will be hard to remove from pan.

3 Cover muffin tin with plastic wrap and refrigerate 2 hours to firm up crab cake mixture.

4 After chilling is complete, heat a 10-inch skillet over medium-low heat and add oil.

5 Fill a shallow dish with panko. Carefully unmold crab cakes from pan and gently roll each cake in panko.

6 Test oil by dropping a pinch of panko into pan. It should sizzle.

7 Fry crab cakes in hot oil 1½–3 minutes per side until cakes are golden brown.

8 Transfer cakes to a paper towel–lined plate to drain. Let cool 3 minutes before serving.

Chili's Boneless Wings

Chili's serves these spicy breaded chicken chunks with celery sticks and blue cheese, just like with their famous bone-in wings.

SERVES 2

2 teaspoons salt

½ teaspoon ground black pepper

¼ teaspoon cayenne pepper

1 cup all-purpose flour

¼ teaspoon paprika

1 large egg

1 cup whole milk

2 boneless, skinless chicken breasts, cut into 2-inch × 1-inch pieces

Vegetable oil, for frying

¼ cup buffalo wing sauce

1 tablespoon margarine

RECIPE VARIATIONS

You can also buy frozen chicken nuggets to make this recipe. Cook nuggets according to package directions and then toss them in the sauce. For a lower-calorie option, use grilled chicken breast and skip the breading step.

1 In a medium bowl, combine salt, black pepper, cayenne pepper, flour, and paprika.

2 In another medium bowl, whisk together egg and milk.

3 Dip chicken pieces in egg mixture, then in flour mixture. Repeat until each chicken piece is double coated.

4 Arrange chicken pieces on a plate and chill in refrigerator 15 minutes.

5 Fill deep fryer with oil per manufacturer directions and heat to 350°F, or in a 5½-quart Dutch oven add enough oil to fill pot by 3 inches, leaving at least 3 inches of space at the top, and place over medium-high heat until oil reaches 350°F.

6 Add chicken 5 or 6 pieces at a time to hot oil and fry 5–6 minutes until breading is golden brown. Transfer to a paper towel–lined plate to drain.

7 In a small microwave-safe bowl, combine hot sauce and margarine. Microwave 20–30 seconds, just until margarine has melted.

8 Place chicken pieces in a container with a lid. Pour prepared sauce over chicken, attach lid, and shake gently until each piece of chicken is coated with sauce. Serve.

CHILI'S BONELESS WINGS

Chili's Southwestern Eggrolls

This recipe has an assortment of traditional Southwestern-style ingredients like black beans, corn, and jalapeños wrapped inside tortillas and deep-fried.

1 (16-ounce) can black beans, rinsed and drained

1 (16-ounce) can corn, rinsed and drained

2 cups fresh spinach, washed and drained

2 medium jalapeños, chopped

2 cloves garlic, pressed in a garlic press

¼ cup chopped fresh cilantro

¼ cup minced yellow onion

½ teaspoon chili powder

½ teaspoon salt

¼ teaspoon ground black pepper

2 cups grated Mexican cheese blend

15 (6-inch) whole-wheat tortillas

½ cup vegetable oil

½ cup prepared salsa

½ cup full-fat sour cream

1 In a large mixing bowl, combine beans, corn, spinach, jalapeños, garlic, cilantro, onion, chili powder, salt, pepper, and cheese and mix well.

2 Place 2 tablespoons mixture on each tortilla and roll into an egg-roll shape.

3 Heat a 10-inch skillet over medium-high heat. Using 1 tablespoon oil per 2 or 3 eggrolls, shallow fry eggrolls in pan until golden brown, then transfer to paper towel–lined plate to drain.

4 Garnish with salsa and sour cream. Serve immediately.

Chili's Texas Cheese Fries

SERVES 4

Once you make these you will come back to this recipe time after time. They are served in the restaurant with ranch salad dressing for dipping, but you can also use sour cream.

½ (28-ounce) bag frozen steak fries

4 strips thick-cut smoked bacon

1 (8-ounce) bag shredded mild Cheddar cheese

¼ cup pickled jalapeño pepper slices

½ cup ranch salad dressing

1 Spread fries evenly over an ungreased half sheet pan and bake according to package directions.

2 Line strips of bacon on another ungreased half sheet pan and bake 15–20 minutes until crispy.

3 Add a thick layer of cheese and jalapeños on top of cooked fries, then crumble bacon on top.

4 Return fries to oven and bake 8–10 minutes until cheese melts. Serve immediately with ranch dressing for dipping.

Chipotle Guacamole

YIELDS 1 CUP
(¼ CUP PER SERVING)

MAKING GUACAMOLE AHEAD

If you want to make guacamole up to a day ahead of time, prepare as directed in the recipe. Transfer to an airtight container, spritz 1 teaspoon lime juice over top, and press plastic wrap directly onto guacamole. Place lid on container and refrigerate until ready to enjoy.

The secret to this guacamole is to gently mash the onion, jalapeño, cilantro, lime, and salt to help release their flavors before adding the avocado. Be sure to use ripe avocados for the best texture.

2 tablespoons minced red onion

2 tablespoons chopped fresh cilantro

1 tablespoon minced jalapeño

1 tablespoon fresh lime juice

¼ teaspoon salt

2 large ripe Hass avocados

1 In a medium bowl, add onion, cilantro, jalapeño, lime juice, and salt. With a wooden spoon, gently mash ingredients five or six times.

2 Slice open avocados, remove pits, and scoop flesh into bowl. With a potato masher, mash until avocado is mostly smooth with some small chunks remaining. Serve immediately.

Chipotle Queso Blanco

Chipotle introduced an all-natural queso in 2017 and then three years later reformulated the recipe to make it smoother and creamier and called it "Queso Blanco." This dip is great with warm tortilla chips!

1 tablespoon unsalted butter

¼ cup finely chopped yellow onion

½ medium jalapeño, minced

½ clove garlic, minced

¼ cup drained canned diced green chilies

1 tablespoon chopped chipotle pepper in adobo

1 cup whole milk

½ cup heavy cream

1 teaspoon cornstarch

1 cup shredded white American cheese

½ cup shredded white Cheddar cheese

½ cup shredded Monterey jack cheese

1 In a 2-quart saucepan over medium heat, add butter. Once butter is melted and foaming, add onion and jalapeño. Sauté, stirring often, 2 minutes, then add garlic, green chilies, and chipotle in adobo and cook 30 seconds.

2 Stir in milk, then reduce heat to medium-low.

3 Whisk together cream and cornstarch in a small bowl until smooth and then whisk into milk in pan. Increase heat to medium and cook, stirring constantly, until mixture comes to a simmer, about 5 minutes.

4 Reduce heat to low and whisk in cheeses. Once smooth, remove from heat and serve immediately.

SERVES 6

CHIPOTLE

Chipotle Mexican Grill currently has over 3,000 locations and has been a leader in promoting organic ingredients. Their restaurants have served more naturally raised meat than any other chain in the US.

Dave & Buster's Pretzel Dogs

SERVES 8

Dave & Buster's popular Pretzel Dogs use all-beef franks for an extra-savory flavor. If making these for a party, cut the finished dogs in half for a fun finger food.

½ cup honey mustard dressing

¼ cup mayonnaise

1 tablespoon habanero hot sauce

¼ teaspoon garlic powder

8 frozen dinner rolls, thawed

8 all-beef hot dogs

3 quarts water

⅓ cup baking soda

2 teaspoons pretzel salt

2 tablespoons unsalted butter, melted

1 In a medium bowl, combine honey mustard dressing, mayonnaise, and hot sauce. Mix well, cover, and chill 1 hour or up to 5 days.

2 Preheat oven to 425°F and line a half baking sheet with parchment.

3 Roll each dinner roll into a 16-inch rope. Wrap each hot dog in a corkscrew fashion with bread dough, pinching ends to secure bread.

4 Add water to a large saucepan over high heat and bring to a boil. Once boiling, add baking soda and stir well. Add 2 or 3 dogs to water at a time and boil 30 seconds. Transfer dogs to prepared baking sheet and sprinkle with pretzel salt.

5 Bake 12–15 minutes until deep golden brown and firm. Remove from oven and brush with butter. Cool 5 minutes before serving with prepared sauce for dipping.

Hooters Original Style Wings

Buffalo chicken wings and ice-cold beer are the most popular items on the menu at Hooters. This recipe makes a big batch for a crowd, which would be a great addition to any party.

SERVES 12

Sauce

3 sticks unsalted butter, softened

½ cup Tabasco sauce

3 tablespoons packed light brown sugar

2 tablespoons chili sauce

1 tablespoon balsamic vinegar

¾ teaspoon salt

¾ teaspoon paprika

⅜ teaspoon cayenne pepper

Wings

3 cups all-purpose flour

2½ teaspoons salt

1 teaspoon paprika

¼ teaspoon cayenne pepper

1 (5-pound bag) whole chicken wings, cut into flats and drumettes

Vegetable oil, for frying

HISTORY OF HOT WINGS

The first spicy chicken wings were served at the Anchor Bar restaurant in Buffalo, New York, in 1964. It is probably one of the most duplicated restaurant recipes in the world.

1 For the sauce: Mix all ingredients together in a medium bowl. Set aside.

2 For the wings: In a large mixing bowl, add flour, salt, paprika, and cayenne pepper and whisk well to combine.

3 Coat flats and drumettes with flour mixture and then refrigerate 90 minutes.

4 Fill deep fryer with oil per manufacturer directions and heat to 350°F, or in a 5½-quart Dutch oven add enough oil to fill pot by 3 inches, leaving at least 3 inches of space at the top, and place over medium-high heat until oil reaches 350°F.

5 Fry wing pieces 4 or 5 at a time 8–10 minutes in hot oil until they are golden brown and reach an internal temperature of 165°F. Place on paper towel–lined plate to remove excess oil.

6 When all wing pieces are fried, place in a large bowl. Add sauce and mix completely. Serve immediately.

LongHorn Steakhouse White Cheddar Stuffed Mushrooms

These mushrooms are stuffed with a rich cheese filling and served in a pool of rich cheese sauce. You can stuff the mushrooms up to 1 day ahead, then cover and refrigerate before baking.

16 large button mushrooms, stems removed

½ block cream cheese, room temperature

½ cup shredded white Cheddar cheese

1 tablespoon chopped fresh chives

¼ teaspoon garlic powder

¼ teaspoon onion powder

¼ teaspoon dried thyme

¼ cup panko bread crumbs

3 tablespoons salted butter, divided

1 cup heavy cream

½ cup grated Parmesan cheese

½ teaspoon ground black pepper

1   Preheat oven to 375°F. Line a half baking sheet with parchment.

2   Place mushrooms top side down on baking sheet. Set aside.

3   In a medium bowl, add cream cheese, Cheddar, chives, garlic powder, onion powder, and thyme. Using a hand mixer, beat on low speed until just combined, then increase speed to medium and beat 30 seconds. Divide mixture evenly between mushroom caps. Refrigerate 10 minutes.

4   Place panko in a small microwave-safe bowl. Add 1 tablespoon butter. Microwave 30 seconds, then stir to coat panko in butter. Divide panko over top of mushrooms.

5   Bake mushrooms 15–20 minutes until tender.

6   While mushrooms cook, add cream and remaining butter to a 10-inch skillet over medium heat. Heat until cream simmers and butter has melted. Reduce heat to low and whisk in Parmesan cheese and pepper. Continue to whisk until cheese is melted and sauce is smooth. Set aside.

7   To serve, pour prepared sauce into a serving dish. Place mushrooms over sauce. Serve hot.

Olive Garden Breadsticks

Many people crave the breadsticks at Olive Garden, and now you can make them at home in almost no time at all. Serve these with the Olive Garden House Salad from Chapter 4 for a tasty lunch!

1 (10.5-ounce/6 count) package frozen breadsticks

2 tablespoons unsalted butter, melted

¼ cup Parmesan cheese

1 Preheat oven to 350°F.

2 Brush each breadstick with butter. Sprinkle top of each breadstick with Parmesan cheese and wrap breadsticks in foil.

3 Bake directly on oven rack 12–15 minutes until breadsticks are hot. Unwrap and serve immediately.

SERVES 6

DIPPING SAUCES

Olive Garden serves dipping sauces for an extra charge. To get the restaurant feel, place warm bowls of marinara and Alfredo sauce on the table for dipping.

Olive Garden Toasted Ravioli

SERVES 4

One of the most popular appetizers on the Olive Garden menu. Serve these with warm marinara sauce for dipping.

¼ cup water

2 large eggs

1 teaspoon Italian seasoning

1 teaspoon garlic salt

1 cup plain bread crumbs

1 cup all-purpose flour

Vegetable oil, for frying

1 (16-ounce) package meat-filled ravioli

1 In a small bowl, mix water and eggs and beat well. Set aside.

2 In a separate small bowl, mix Italian seasoning and garlic salt with bread crumbs and set aside.

3 In a third small bowl, add flour and set aside.

4 Fill deep fryer with oil per manufacturer directions and heat to 350°F, or in a 5½-quart Dutch oven add enough oil to fill pot by 3 inches, leaving at least 3 inches of space at the top, and place over medium-high heat until oil reaches 350°F.

5 Dip ravioli in flour, then in eggs, then in bread crumbs and carefully place in hot oil.

6 Fry ravioli in batches of 3 or 4 about 2–3 minutes until golden, remove from oil, and drain on a paper towel–lined plate. Continue with remaining ravioli. Serve warm.

Outback Steakhouse Bloomin' Onion

The Bloomin' Onion from Outback Steakhouse may be one of the most popular appetizers in America; millions are sold every year.

SERVES 4

Sauce

½ cup mayonnaise

2 teaspoons ketchup

2 tablespoons cream-style horseradish

¼ teaspoon paprika

¼ teaspoon salt

⅛ teaspoon dried oregano

⅛ teaspoon ground black pepper

⅛ teaspoon cayenne pepper

Seasoned Flour

1 cup all-purpose flour

2 teaspoons paprika

1 teaspoon garlic powder

¼ teaspoon ground black pepper

⅛ teaspoon cayenne pepper

Batter

¼ cup cornstarch

¾ cup all-purpose flour

1 teaspoon minced garlic

1 teaspoon paprika

½ teaspoon salt

½ teaspoon ground black pepper

12 ounces beer

1 large Vidalia or Texas sweet onion

2–4 cups vegetable oil

1 For the sauce: In a small bowl, mix together all ingredients. Cover and refrigerate until ready to serve.

2 For the seasoned flour: In a shallow bowl, combine all ingredients and whisk well.

3 For the batter: In a large bowl, whisk cornstarch, flour, garlic, paprika, salt, and pepper until well blended. Add beer and whisk until smooth.

4 Cut about ¾ inch off top of onion and peel. Place onion cut-side down and cut 12 vertical wedges around the root of onion. Do not cut through the bottom root end. Remove about 1 inch of petals from center of onion and gently separate onion petals.

5 Fill deep fryer with oil per manufacturer directions and heat to 375°F, and place over medium-high heat until oil reaches 375°F.

6 Dip prepared onion in seasoned flour mixture. Shake off excess. Separate petals and dip in batter to coat thoroughly, making sure batter gets between petals. Return onion to seasoned flour mixture and toss to coat; make sure flour gets between petals and coats them evenly.

7 Gently place onion in fryer basket root-side down and deep-fry 1½ minutes. Turn onion over and fry an additional 2 minutes or until golden brown. Drain on paper towels.

8 Place onion upright in a shallow bowl and remove center core with a circular cutter or apple corer. Place a small ramekin in center of onion and spoon prepared sauce into ramekin. Serve immediately.

OUTBACK STEAKHOUSE BLOOMIN' ONION

Papa Johns Garlic Knots

Garlic knots make a tasty side for your favorite pizza, pasta, or even steak dinner. They can also be a snack or served as an appetizer for a party.

SERVES 4

16 ounces prepared refrigerated pizza dough

1 stick unsalted butter, melted

½ teaspoon garlic powder

½ teaspoon Italian seasoning

½ cup grated Parmesan cheese

1 Let dough warm up to room temperature 30 minutes. Divide dough into eight equal pieces and roll each piece into a 6-inch rope. Tie each rope into a knot. Place knots 2 inches apart on a half sheet pan lined with parchment. Cover with a damp towel and let rise on the countertop 30 minutes.

2 Preheat oven to 425°F.

3 In a small bowl, combine butter, garlic, and Italian seasoning. Mix well.

4 Once knots are puffed, remove towel. Brush knots with half the butter mixture.

5 Bake 10–11 minutes until knots are golden brown on top and bottom. Remove from oven and brush with remaining butter mixture and sprinkle with Parmesan cheese. Cool 5 minutes before serving.

Papa Johns Italian Papadia

Refrigerated pizza dough is a great shortcut ingredient found in the deli department of most grocery stores and makes this a meal you can enjoy any night of the week.

8 ounces prepared refrigerated pizza dough

⅓ cup barbecue sauce, divided

½ cup shredded mozzarella cheese

¼ cup shredded Monterey jack cheese

¼ cup shredded smoked Gouda cheese

2 strips thick-cut smoked bacon, cooked crisp and chopped

6 ounces grilled chicken breast strips

¼ cup thin-sliced yellow onion

1 tablespoon olive oil

2 tablespoons grated Parmesan cheese

1 Preheat oven to 450°F and line a half sheet pan with parchment.

2 Bring pizza dough to room temperature. On a lightly floured surface, roll dough into a 12-inch circle. Transfer to prepared pan.

3 Spread half of barbecue sauce over half of pizza crust. Top with mozzarella, Monterey jack, and Gouda cheeses, bacon, chicken, and onion. Drizzle with remaining barbecue sauce. Fold dough over, encasing the fillings, but do not crimp edges. Brush dough with olive oil and sprinkle with Parmesan cheese.

4 Bake 20 minutes or until pizza crust is golden and fillings are melted. Let cool 5 minutes before slicing in half and serving.

Texas Roadhouse Rolls with Honey Cinnamon Butter

These rolls are fluffy, buttery, and delicious served warm with a scoop of lightly sweet butter flavored with cinnamon.

YIELDS 12 ROLLS AND 1½ CUPS BUTTER (1 ROLL AND 1½ TABLESPOONS BUTTER PER SERVING)

Rolls

¾ cups whole milk

¼ cup granulated sugar

¾ teaspoon dry active yeast

1 large egg, room temperature

1 stick unsalted butter, melted and cooled

½ teaspoon salt

1½ cups all-purpose flour

1½ cups bread flour

Cinnamon Butter

1 cup softened unsalted butter

¼ cup sweetened condensed milk

2 tablespoons honey

1 teaspoon ground cinnamon

1 For the rolls: Heat milk in a small microwave-safe bowl on high 20 seconds. Stir in sugar and yeast and allow to stand until yeast is bubbling and foamy, about 10 minutes.

2 In a large bowl using a wooden spoon, add yeast mixture, egg, and butter. Stir in the salt and flour until it forms a shaggy ball, then knead on a lightly floured surface by hand until dough is smooth, about 10 minutes.

3 Form dough into a smooth ball, cover bowl with a damp towel, and let rise in a draft-free spot 1 hour or until doubled in bulk.

4 Preheat oven to 375°F and line a half sheet pan with parchment.

5 Turn out dough onto a lightly floured surface. Press out any air bubbles with your palm. Shape dough into an 8-inch × 12-inch rectangle. Cut dough into twelve squares.

6 Transfer dough squares to prepared baking sheet at least 1 inch apart. Cover with a damp towel and allow to rise 30–40 minutes until rolls are puffy and a finger pressed into the side leaves a mark.

7 Bake 18–20 minutes until rolls are golden brown on top and bottom. Cool on sheet pan 10 minutes before serving.

8 For the cinnamon butter: Place all ingredients in a food processor. Blend until smooth.

TGI Fridays Loaded Potato Skins

SERVES 5

TGI FRIDAYS HISTORY OF FIRSTS

TGI Fridays has a long history of innovation in the restaurant industry. They have been credited with naming happy hour, being the first restaurant chain to serve nonalcoholic drinks, and popularizing loaded potato skins.

While hotly contested, TGI Fridays claim they invented loaded potato skins in 1974 when a cook deep-fried leftover potato skins from making mashed potatoes. He added seasoning and toppings and a legend was (allegedly) born!

10 baked potato halves

1 tablespoon unsalted butter, melted

½ teaspoon salt

¾ cup shredded sharp Cheddar cheese

5 strips thick-cut smoked bacon, cooked crisp and crumbled

½ cup full-fat sour cream

1 medium green onion, green section thinly sliced

1 Preheat oven to 375°F.

2 Remove flesh from potato halves, leaving ¼ inch of flesh inside skin. Reserve flesh for another use.

3 Brush potato shells with butter and season with salt. Place on an ungreased half sheet pan. Bake 15–20 minutes until crisp.

4 Remove potato skins and sprinkle with cheese and bacon. Return to oven 6–8 minutes until cheese has melted.

5 Serve potato skins with sour cream and green onions. Serve hot.

TGI FRIDAYS LOADED POTATO SKINS

Tommy Bahama Coconut Crusted Crab Cakes

SERVES 4

Designed to be a place that served the food and drink the fictional Tommy Bahama would enjoy, Tommy Bahama restaurants opened in 1996. The concept is popular with customers who also appreciate the beach lifestyle!

1 pound lump crabmeat, drained and checked for shells

¼ cup shredded unsweetened coconut

2 tablespoons finely chopped green onion

2 tablespoons minced yellow onion

2 tablespoons panko bread crumbs

2 tablespoons all-purpose flour

1 large egg, beaten

1 tablespoon mayonnaise

1 teaspoon Old Bay Seasoning

1 teaspoon ground black pepper

½ tablespoon salt

¼ cup vegetable oil

⅓ cup Thai sweet chili sauce

1 In a medium bowl, combine all ingredients except oil and Thai sweet chili sauce. Mix gently until combined, making sure not to break up the crabmeat. Portion crabmeat mixture into four patties.

2 In a 10-inch cast iron skillet over medium heat, add oil. Once hot, add patties. Cook 4 minutes per side or until golden brown and crisp. Transfer to a paper towel lined–plate to drain.

3 Serve hot with Thai sweet chili sauce for dipping.

CHAPTER 4

Soup and Salad

APPLEBEE'S ORIENTAL CHICKEN SALAD

Applebee's Oriental Chicken Salad

What makes this salad recipe so delicious is the tangy Asian salad dressing that can be doubled and kept in the refrigerator for up to 2 weeks. This is sure to become one of your favorite dinner salads.

4 frozen breaded chicken tenderloins

6 tablespoons honey

3 tablespoons rice vinegar

½ cup mayonnaise

2 teaspoons Dijon mustard

¼ teaspoon sesame oil

2 cups chopped green cabbage

2 cups chopped red cabbage

6 cups chopped romaine lettuce

1 medium carrot, shredded

2 medium green onions, chopped

¼ cup toasted sliced almonds

⅔ cup fried chow mein noodles

1 Preheat oven and cook chicken tenders according to package directions. Once cooked, cut tenders into ½-inch pieces.

2 While tenders are cooking combine honey, vinegar, mayonnaise, mustard, and sesame oil in a small bowl. Stir well and chill in refrigerator until ready to serve.

3 In a large bowl, combine green cabbage, red cabbage, lettuce, carrot, green onions, almonds, and fried noodles. Toss with prepared dressing. Divide between four serving plates and top each with chicken. Serve immediately.

California Pizza Kitchen Dakota Smashed Pea + Barley Soup

SERVES 8

This unique soup is full of flavor and is a signature dish at CPK. You can easily make it vegetarian by swapping the chicken broth for vegetable broth.

2 cups split peas, rinsed and drained

8 cups water, divided

4 cups chicken broth

$\frac{1}{3}$ cup minced onion

1 large clove garlic, minced

2 teaspoons lemon juice

1 teaspoon salt

1 teaspoon granulated sugar

$\frac{1}{4}$ teaspoon dried parsley

$\frac{1}{4}$ teaspoon ground white pepper

$\frac{1}{8}$ teaspoon dried thyme

$\frac{1}{2}$ cup barley

2 medium carrots, diced

$\frac{1}{2}$ medium stalk celery, diced

1 To a 3-quart saucepan add split peas to a large pot with 6 cups water, chicken broth, onion, garlic, lemon juice, salt, sugar, parsley, pepper, and thyme. Stir well, then bring to a boil over high heat. Reduce heat to medium-low and simmer 75 minutes or until peas are soft.

2 While peas are cooking, combine barley with remaining water in a 1-quart saucepan. Bring to a boil over high heat, reduce heat to medium-low, and simmer 75 minutes or until barley is soft and most of water has been absorbed.

3 Drain barley in a colander and add to split peas. Add carrots and celery and continue to simmer soup 15–30 minutes until carrots are tender. Stir occasionally.

4 Turn off heat, cover soup, and let sit 10–15 minutes before serving.

California Pizza Kitchen Italian Chopped Salad

This salad is like the best-ever Italian sub sandwich in a bowl. This could be a great recipe for using leftover turkey breast after the holidays, or you could use your favorite roasted turkey breast lunch meat.

SERVES 4

Dressing

½ cup extra-virgin olive oil

¼ cup red wine vinegar

3 tablespoons grated Parmesan cheese

2 tablespoons Dijon mustard

1 teaspoon Italian seasoning

½ teaspoon dried oregano

¼ teaspoon ground black pepper

¼ teaspoon salt

Salad

1 medium head iceberg lettuce, chopped

1 medium romaine heart, chopped

4 basil leaves, chopped

6 ounces dry Italian salami, cut into strips

1 cup canned garbanzo beans

2 Roma tomatoes, seeded and diced

2 cups chopped turkey breast

1 cup shredded mozzarella cheese

2 medium green onions, green part only, thinly sliced

1 For the dressing: In a pint jar with a lid, add all ingredients. Shake 30 seconds. Set aside.

2 For the salad: In a large bowl, add all ingredients except green onions. Toss well. Shake dressing again and add half to salad. Toss to coat, adding more dressing if desired. Garnish with green onions and serve immediately.

California Pizza Kitchen Thai Crunch Salad

SERVES 4

This salad makes a filling meal for four or an appetizer for eight. If you are sensitive to peanuts, you can make the dressing for this salad with sunflower butter.

Dressing

¼ cup creamy peanut butter

3 tablespoons rice vinegar

2 tablespoons vegetable oil

1 tablespoon light soy sauce

1 tablespoon lime juice

1 tablespoon honey

2 teaspoons sesame oil

⅛ teaspoon ground ginger

⅛ teaspoon ground black pepper

⅛ teaspoon crushed red pepper flakes

Salad

4 ounces thin rice noodles

½ cup vegetable oil

6 cups shredded napa cabbage

2 cups shredded red cabbage

1 cup shelled edamame

½ cup julienned carrot

½ cup chopped English cucumber

½ cup chopped fresh cilantro

2 medium green onions, chopped

2 cups grilled chicken breast strips

½ cup wonton strips

½ cup roasted unsalted peanuts, lightly crushed

1 For the dressing: In a blender, add all ingredients. Purée 20 seconds, then transfer to a small bowl and chill until ready to use.

2 For the salad: Break rice noodles into 2- to 3-inch pieces.

3 In a 2-quart saucepan, add vegetable oil. Heat over medium-high heat until oil reaches 350°F. Add half of noodles to oil and cook 10 seconds, then flip and cook 10 seconds more or until noodles are puffed. Remove noodles from oil to a paper towel–lined plate to drain. Repeat with remaining noodles. Set aside.

4 In a large bowl, combine napa cabbage, red cabbage, edamame, carrot, cucumber, cilantro, and green onions and toss well to combine. Add half of dressing, chicken, and wonton strips and toss to distribute. Add more dressing as desired.

5 Divide salad between serving plates. Top with peanuts and fried rice noodles. Serve immediately.

Chick-fil-A Cobb Salad

The Chick-fil-A Cobb Salad comes with their popular Avocado Lime Ranch Dressing and crispy bell peppers for a hint of crunch. It can be customized with a variety of their popular chicken options.

SERVES 4

⅓ cup plus ¼ cup low-fat buttermilk, divided

⅓ cup mayonnaise

½ large avocado

1 tablespoon fresh lime juice

2 teaspoons chopped fresh chives

2 teaspoons chopped fresh dill

1 teaspoon onion powder

¼ teaspoon garlic powder

⅛ teaspoon plus ½ teaspoon salt, divided

⅛ teaspoon plus 1 teaspoon ground black pepper, divided

2 (6-ounce) boneless, skinless chicken breast fillets

2 tablespoons dill pickle brine

1 teaspoon granulated sugar

Vegetable oil, for frying

½ cup all-purpose flour

½ teaspoon paprika

6 cups chopped romaine lettuce

4 cups spring mix

1 cup frozen fire-roasted corn, thawed

1 cup whole grape tomatoes

½ cup crumbled cooked bacon

½ cup shredded Monterrey jack cheese, divided

½ cup shredded Cheddar cheese, divided

2 large hardboiled eggs, sliced

½ cup Fresh Gourmet Crispy Red Peppers

(continued)

1 In a blender, add ⅓ cup buttermilk, mayonnaise, and avocado. Purée until smooth, then transfer to a small bowl and add lime juice, chives, dill, onion powder, garlic powder, ⅛ teaspoon salt, and ⅛ teaspoon pepper and mix well. Cover and chill until ready to serve.

2 In a large resealable plastic bag, add chicken, ¼ cup buttermilk, pickle brine, and sugar. After removing as much air as you can, seal the bag and massage to evenly coat chicken and combine marinade ingredients. Refrigerate at least 2 hours or up to 24 hours.

3 Remove chicken from refrigerator 30 minutes before cooking to warm to room temperature.

4 Fill deep fryer with oil per manufacturer directions and heat to 350°F, or in a 5½-quart Dutch oven add enough oil to fill pot by 3 inches, leaving at least 3 inches of space at the top, and place over medium-high heat until oil reaches 350°F.

5 In a medium bowl, add flour, 1 teaspoon pepper, ½ teaspoon salt, and paprika and mix well to combine. Remove chicken from marinade and let excess drip off. Dredge chicken in flour mixture, shaking off excess flour, and gently place in hot oil. Fry 5–7 minutes until chicken reaches an internal temperature of 165°F. Remove chicken from oil and let drain on a paper towel–lined plate.

6 In a large bowl, combine romaine, spring mix, corn, tomatoes, bacon, and ¼ cup each Monterrey jack and Cheddar cheeses. Toss well to mix.

7 Slice chicken breasts into ½-inch strips.

8 Divide salad mixture between serving plates. Top salads with chicken strips, sliced egg, crispy red peppers, and remaining cheese. Drizzle with prepared dressing. Serve immediately.

Chili's Chicken Enchilada Soup

Popular as an appetizer or as a side, this soup is rich and creamy and has all the best flavors of chicken enchiladas. Be sure to garnish bowls with shredded cheese and crumbled tortilla chips like they do in the restaurant.

1 tablespoon vegetable oil

1 pound boneless, skinless chicken breast

½ cup diced yellow onion

1 clove garlic, finely minced

4 cups chicken broth

1 cup masa harina

3 cups water, divided

1 cup enchilada sauce

16 ounces Velveeta cheese

1 teaspoon salt

1 teaspoon chili powder

½ teaspoon ground cumin

1 cup shredded Cheddar cheese

1 cup crumbled corn tortilla chips

SERVES 12

TRY A ROTISSERIE CHICKEN

If you are in a hurry, you could buy a cooked rotisserie chicken from the grocery store for this recipe. Ready-to-eat rotisserie chickens are great for sandwiches, soups, stews, and casseroles.

1 In a 3-quart saucepan over medium heat, add oil. Add chicken breasts and brown 4–5 minutes per side. Set chicken aside.

2 Add onion and garlic to pan and sauté over medium heat 2 minutes or until onion begins to be translucent. Add chicken broth and stir well to release any brown bits from bottom of pan.

3 In a medium bowl, combine masa harina with 2 cups water and whisk until blended. Add masa mixture to pan, then add onion, garlic, and broth and whisk until smooth.

4 Add remaining water, enchilada sauce, Velveeta cheese, salt, chili powder, and cumin to pan and bring to a boil.

5 Shred chicken into bite-sized pieces and add to pan. Reduce heat to low and simmer 30–40 minutes until thick. Serve hot with Cheddar and tortilla chips for garnish.

LongHorn Steakhouse Loaded Potato Soup

SERVES 8

Loaded Potato Soup is a popular appetizer at LongHorn Steakhouse and is made without flour so is gluten-free. Here, Yukon gold potatoes are used to add buttery flavor and a creamy texture.

4 strips thick-cut smoked bacon

2 tablespoons unsalted butter

½ yellow onion, peeled and finely chopped

1 clove garlic, minced

2 cups chicken broth

2 cups water

6 cups diced peeled Yukon gold potatoes

½ teaspoon salt

½ teaspoon ground black pepper

1 cup heavy cream

2 cups shredded sharp Cheddar cheese, divided

2 medium green onions, thinly sliced

1 In a 3-quart saucepan over medium heat, fry bacon until crisp, about 8 minutes. Remove bacon with a slotted spoon and transfer to a paper towel–lined plate to drain.

2 To same pan over medium heat, stir in butter until melted. Add yellow onion and sauté until tender, about 4 minutes. Add garlic and cook 30 seconds.

3 Add chicken broth, water, and potatoes. Bring to a boil, then reduce heat to medium-low and simmer 15 minutes, stirring often.

4 After 15 minutes, check potatoes to see if they are tender. A fork should slide in and out of potato dices easily. Transfer 3 cups potato dices from pan into a medium bowl. With an immersion blender, purée soup in pan until smooth.

5 With blender running, add salt, pepper, and cream. Remove blender and whisk in 1 cup Cheddar cheese until melted and combined. Return potato dices to pan and stir well.

6 Divide soup between serving bowls. Top with crumbled bacon, remaining Cheddar cheese, and green onions. Serve hot.

O'Charley's Black & Bleu Caesar

If you want a hearty and filling entrée salad, O'Charley's makes one of the best using fan-sliced steak and blue cheese.

SERVES 1

1 (6-ounce) sirloin steak

2 tablespoons salted butter, melted

1 tablespoon Cajun seasoning

3½ cups chopped romaine lettuce

1¼ cups shredded Parmesan cheese, divided

1¼ cups large croutons, divided

¼ cup Caesar dressing

3 (¼-inch) slices Roma tomato

¼ cup crumbled blue cheese

¼ cup diced cooked bacon

1 Preheat grill to 350°F.

2 Brush steak on both sides with butter and sprinkle with Cajun seasoning.

3 Place steak on grill and cook 2 minutes, then turn and cook 2–3 minutes more to the desired degree of doneness. Cut into ½-inch slices.

4 In a large bowl, add romaine and then sprinkle half of Parmesan cheese and half of croutons over top. Add dressing and toss well.

5 Place salad in a chilled serving bowl and sprinkle with remaining Parmesan cheese. Add tomato slices and top with fan-sliced steak, blue cheese, bacon, and remaining croutons. Serve immediately.

O'CHARLEY'S BLACK & BLEU CAESAR

O'Charley's Loaded Potato Soup

A one-of-a-kind signature soup from O'Charley's sure to make you happy. It is full of beloved flavors like Cheddar cheese, chives, and crumbled bacon.

3 pounds red potatoes, peeled and diced into ½-inch cubes

¼ cup melted margarine

¼ cup all-purpose flour

8 cups half-and-half

1 (16-ounce) block Velveeta cheese, melted

½ teaspoon garlic powder

1 teaspoon hot pepper sauce

6 strips thick-cut smoked bacon, cooked crisp and crumbled

½ cup shredded Cheddar cheese

½ cup chopped fresh parsley

½ cup chopped fresh chives

1 Place potatoes in a 3-quart saucepan, cover with water, and boil over high heat 10 minutes or until tender.

2 In a 2-quart saucepan over low heat, combine margarine and flour. Stir constantly, gradually adding half-and-half, until liquid begins to thicken, about 5–7 minutes. Add Velveeta cheese and stir well.

3 Drain potatoes and add to Velveeta mixture. Stir in garlic powder and hot pepper sauce. Cover and cook over low heat 30 minutes, stirring occasionally.

4 Transfer to individual serving bowls and top with crumbled bacon, Cheddar, parsley, and chives.

ABOUT O'CHARLEY'S

O'Charley's is a casual-dining family restaurant chain with over sixty locations in thirteen states. They serve freshly prepared steaks grilled to perfection, seafood, chicken, salads, desserts, and more. Loaded Potato Soup is one of their most popular menu items, and the recipe is one that many people have tried to re-create.

Olive Garden Chicken & Gnocchi Soup

SERVES 6

WHAT IS GNOCCHI?

Gnocchi is an Italian dumpling. Most gnocchi are potato based, but they can be made with semolina or polenta flour. Gnocchi are eaten as entrées or used as alternatives to pasta in soups. They are widely available dried, frozen, or fresh in vacuum-sealed packages in supermarkets and specialty stores.

Chicken & Gnocchi Soup is one of the most popular soups on the menu at Olive Garden. Look for premade gnocchi in the frozen food section of your local supermarket.

⅓ cup salted butter

2 cloves garlic, minced

1 pound cubed chicken breast

⅓ cup all-purpose flour

½ teaspoon ground black pepper

2 cups whole milk

2 cups heavy cream

½ medium carrot, shredded

1 medium stalk celery, shredded

¼ cup shredded yellow onion

½ cup torn fresh spinach

3 chicken bouillon cubes

1 (16-ounce) package frozen gnocchi

1 In a 3-quart saucepan over medium heat, melt butter. Add garlic and sauté 2–3 minutes. Add chicken and cook 8–10 minutes until chicken is golden brown and reaches an internal temperature of 165°F.

2 Stir in flour and pepper and mix well. Cook 2–3 minutes until flour is cooked into chicken. Add milk and cream and stir well.

3 Add carrot, celery, onion, and spinach. Drop bouillon cubes into pot. Mix ingredients well, stirring occasionally. Cover and simmer 10 minutes.

4 Add gnocchi to pan. Cook 3–4 minutes more, until gnocchi is done. Serve hot.

Olive Garden House Salad

This classic Italian salad is sure to be a hit with friends and family. Serve it with breadsticks and soup to create a true Olive Garden meal at home.

SERVES 2

Dressing
¼ cup mayonnaise

¼ cup olive oil

2 tablespoons white wine vinegar

2 tablespoons corn syrup

2 tablespoons Parmesan cheese

2 tablespoons Romano cheese

¼ teaspoon garlic salt

½ teaspoon Italian seasoning

1 tablespoon lemon juice

Salad
1 (12-ounce) bag American Blend salad mix

10 (⅛-inch) slices red onion

10 black olives

8 pepperoncini peppers

1 medium tomato, sliced

1 cup croutons

SOUP, SALAD, AND BREADSTICKS

One of the most popular promotions at Olive Garden is their weekday unlimited Soup AND Salad AND Breadsticks lunch special. Or, for dinner when you order an entrée at Olive Garden, you can also enjoy Never-Ending Soup or Salad and Breadsticks!

1 For the dressing: Place all ingredients in a blender. Blend until combined well. Refrigerate until ready to use.

2 For the salad: Combine all ingredients except croutons in a medium bowl with a lid.

3 Refrigerate salad, covered, 1–2 hours. Place salad plates in freezer to chill.

4 When ready to serve, add dressing to salad and toss well to coat, then top with croutons. Divide salad between chilled plates and serve immediately.

Olive Garden Pasta e Fagioli Soup

SERVES 8

OLIVE GARDEN TRAINING IN TUSCANY

Did you know that Olive Garden sends select managers and cooks to Tuscany every year to train? While they have advertised a Tuscany Institute, the reality is less glamorous. Still, employees do train in Italy to learn about Italian cooking and hospitality!

"Pasta e fagioli" means "pasta and beans" in Italian, and Italian peasants have served this traditionally meatless soup for centuries. This recipe, re-creating Olive Garden's, contains ground beef, but it can be omitted and vegetable stock swapped for meat stock to make a vegetarian dish.

2 pounds 90/10 ground beef

1 medium yellow onion, peeled and chopped

3 medium carrots, chopped

4 medium stalks celery, chopped

2 (28-ounce) cans undrained diced tomatoes

1 (16-ounce) can red kidney beans, drained and rinsed

1 (16-ounce) can white kidney beans, drained and rinsed

3 (10-ounce) cans beef stock

3 teaspoons dried oregano

2 teaspoons ground black pepper

5 teaspoons dried parsley

1 teaspoon Tabasco sauce

1 (20-ounce) jar spaghetti sauce

8 ounces dry elbow pasta

1 Add ground beef to a large skillet over medium heat. Use a wooden spoon to break up beef and cook 8–10 minutes, stirring often, until browned. Drain fat from beef and add to a slow cooker.

2 Add remaining ingredients except pasta to slow cooker and stir to combine. Cook on low 7–8 hours or on high 4–5 hours.

3 During last 30 minutes, add pasta and cook on high. Serve hot.

Olive Garden Zuppa Toscana

This is a wonderful soup you can make at home and is one of the most requested restaurant copycat recipes from Olive Garden. If you don't have or don't like kale, try Swiss chard in this recipe instead. Serve with some fresh crusty Italian bread.

SERVES 8

1 pound Italian sausage, crumbled

½ pound thick-cut smoked bacon, chopped

1 large yellow onion, peeled and chopped

2 large russet potatoes, diced

2 (14.5-ounce) cans chicken broth

1 quart water

2 cloves garlic, minced

½ teaspoon salt

½ teaspoon ground black pepper

2 cups chopped kale

1 cup heavy cream

1. In a 10-inch skillet over medium heat, add sausage. Cook, stirring occasionally, until well browned, about 8 minutes. Remove from pan and drain on paper towels.
2. To same skillet over medium heat, add bacon and cook until crisp, about 8 minutes. Drain on paper towels.
3. In a 3-quart saucepan over medium heat, add onion, potatoes, broth, water, and garlic. Cook 15 minutes or until potatoes are tender. Add sausage, bacon, salt, and pepper and stir to combine.
4. Reduce heat to low and simmer 10 minutes. Add kale and cream. Heat 5–10 minutes more until kale is wilted. Serve hot.

Panera Bread Broccoli Cheddar Soup

SERVES 8

Serve bowls of this soup with additional shredded Cheddar for a garnish. For a special touch, serve in a warm sourdough bread bowl.

6 tablespoons unsalted butter

1 medium yellow onion, peeled and finely chopped

1 clove garlic, minced

¼ cup all-purpose flour

2 cups chicken broth

2 cups chopped broccoli florets

½ cup finely grated carrot

½ cup finely chopped celery

2 cups half-and-half

¼ cup shredded American cheese

2 cups shredded medium Cheddar cheese

½ teaspoon ground black pepper

¼ teaspoon salt

1 In a 3-quart saucepan over medium heat, add butter. Once melted, add onion. Sauté 5 minutes or until very tender. Add garlic and cook 30 seconds.

2 Sprinkle in flour and cook, stirring constantly, 1 minute. Reduce heat to low and whisk in broth. Once smooth, increase heat to medium and add broccoli, carrot, and celery. Bring mixture to a boil, then reduce heat to medium-low and simmer 10 minutes.

3 After 10 minutes, test that broccoli is tender using a fork; fork should pierce broccoli easily. Stir in half-and-half and American cheese and stir until cheese is melted.

4 Add Cheddar in three intervals, stirring well until each addition is melted before adding more. Stir in salt and pepper. Serve hot.

Panera Bread Fuji Apple Salad with Chicken

Rotisserie chicken breast makes this an easy salad to have for a quick lunch or dinner, and the savory chicken pairs well with the sweet, crisp dry apple.

SERVES 4

Dressing

½ cup vegetable oil

¼ cup apple juice

3 tablespoons white balsamic vinegar

2 tablespoons honey

¼ teaspoon salt

¼ teaspoon onion powder

⅛ teaspoon garlic powder

⅛ teaspoon dried rosemary

Salad

8 cups chopped romaine hearts

4 cups spring mix

2 rotisserie chicken breasts, sliced

¼ cup sliced red onion

½ cup dried apple chips

½ cup crumbled Gorgonzola

½ cup toasted pecans

1 For the dressing: In a pint jar with a lid, add all ingredients. Cover and shake 30 seconds. Set aside.

2 For the salad: In a large bowl, add romaine and spring mix and mix well. Add chicken, onion, and apple chips and toss to mix.

3 Divide salad between serving plates. Garnish with Gorgonzola and pecans. Drizzle with dressing. Serve immediately.

Panera Bread Homestyle Chicken Noodle Soup

SERVES 4

This popular soup is a staple of the Panera menu and wonderful when you need comfort food. If you cannot find curly egg noodles, feel free to use any thick egg noodle you have available.

2 tablespoons vegetable oil

½ cup chopped celery

½ cup chopped carrot

¼ cup chopped yellow onion

½ teaspoon sea salt

½ teaspoon ground black pepper

½ teaspoon poultry seasoning

6 cups chicken bone broth

1 pound boneless, skinless chicken breast

6 ounces curly egg noodles

1 teaspoon fresh lemon juice

1 In a 3-quart saucepan over medium heat, add oil. Once hot, swirl pan to coat and add celery, carrot, and onion. Sauté until tender, about 5 minutes. Add salt, pepper, and poultry seasoning and sauté until spices are fragrant, about 30 seconds.

2 Add bone broth and stir well, then add chicken breast. Increase heat to high. Bring mixture to a boil, then reduce heat to medium-low, cover pan, and cook 15 minutes or until chicken reaches an internal temperature of 165°F in thickest part. Remove chicken from pan and let cool slightly, then shred into large pieces with two forks. Set aside.

3 While chicken cools, return pan to medium heat and add noodles. Cook until noodles are tender, about 8 minutes. Reduce heat to low and add shredded chicken and lemon juice. Serve hot.

PANERA BREAD HOMESTYLE CHICKEN NOODLE SOUP

P.F. Chang's Wonton Soup

SERVES 12

This flavorful soup combines pork wontons, plump shrimp, and cubes of juicy chicken in a savory broth finished with fresh green onion.

Homemade Wontons

½ pound pork, coarsely chopped

8 medium shrimp, peeled and deveined, coarsely chopped

1 teaspoon packed light brown sugar

1 tablespoon Chinese rice wine or dry sherry

1 tablespoon light soy sauce

2 teaspoons finely chopped green onion, divided

1 teaspoon finely chopped fresh ginger

24 wonton wrappers

Soup

4 cups chicken stock

2 boneless, skinless chicken breast halves, cubed

1 pound medium shrimp, peeled and deveined

1 cup torn fresh spinach

1 cup sliced mushrooms

1 (8-ounce) can water chestnuts, drained and rinsed

1 teaspoon packed light brown sugar

1 tablespoon Chinese rice wine or dry sherry

2 tablespoons soy sauce

1 teaspoon diced green onion

1 teaspoon finely chopped fresh ginger

1 For the homemade wontons: In a medium bowl, mix pork and shrimp with brown sugar, rice wine, soy sauce, 1 teaspoon green onion, and ginger. Combine well and set aside 25–30 minutes for flavors to blend.

2 Place 1 teaspoon filling in center of each wonton wrapper. Wet edges of each wonton with a little water and press edges together with your fingers to seal.

3 For the soup: In a 2-quart saucepan over high heat, bring stock to a rolling boil. Add remaining ingredients and boil 10 minutes.

4 Add wontons to boiling chicken stock and cook 4–5 minutes. Transfer to individual soup bowls and serve garnished with remaining green onion.

Red Lobster New England Clam Chowder

This recipe makes a traditional New England clam chowder that is full of vegetables. You can serve it as a side dish, but it is hearty enough to have as a meal along with some Red Lobster Cheddar Bay Biscuits (see Chapter 9).

SERVES 8

2 tablespoons salted butter

1 cup diced yellow onions

½ cup diced celery

½ cup diced leeks

¼ teaspoon chopped garlic

2 tablespoons all-purpose flour

4 cups whole milk

1 cup minced clams with juice

1 cup diced russet potatoes

1 tablespoon salt

1 teaspoon dried thyme

½ cup heavy cream

1 Melt butter in a 3-quart saucepan over medium heat. Add onions, celery, and leeks. Sauté until just tender, about 3–4 minutes. Add garlic and sauté 30 seconds. Remove from heat, add flour, and mix well.

2 Return pan to stove. Add milk and stir. Drain clams and add juice to soup. Increase heat to medium-high and bring to a boil, stirring often. Once boiling, reduce heat to medium-low. Add potatoes, salt, and thyme. Simmer 10 minutes or until potatoes are fork-tender.

3 Add clams and simmer 5 minutes, then remove pan from heat and stir in cream. Serve immediately.

TGI Fridays White Cheddar Broccoli Soup

SERVES 6

A bit of white American cheese will help keep this soup creamy and add an extra depth of flavor. You can get just a few slices from your grocer's deli department.

6 tablespoons unsalted butter

½ cup finely chopped white onion

2 cloves garlic, minced

⅓ cup all-purpose flour

4 cups chicken broth

1 cup water

4½ cups chopped broccoli florets

1 cup half-and-half

4 slices white American cheese

1 cup shredded white Cheddar cheese

½ teaspoon salt

¼ teaspoon ground black pepper

1 cup shredded mild Cheddar cheese

1 In a 3-quart saucepan over medium heat, add butter. Once melted, add onion and sauté until tender, about 5 minutes. Add garlic and cook 30 seconds or until fragrant.

2 Sprinkle flour over onion mixture and cook 1 minute, then reduce heat to low and stir in broth and water. Increase heat to medium and bring mixture to a boil, then reduce heat to medium-low.

3 Add broccoli and simmer 15 minutes or until broccoli is fork-tender.

4 Reduce heat to low. Stir in half-and-half and American cheese and mix until cheese is melted. Stir in white Cheddar cheese until melted, then add salt and pepper. Serve soup hot with mild Cheddar for garnish.

Tommy Bahama Lump Blue Crab Bisque

Founded in 1993 as an "island lifestyle" clothing company for men and women, the Tommy Bahama brand has expanded to include restaurants, cocktail bars, and a line of silver and gold rums.

SERVES 4

4 tablespoons salted butter

½ cup finely minced yellow onion

¼ cup finely minced celery

2 cloves garlic, minced

¼ cup all-purpose flour

1 cup dry white wine

2 cups seafood stock

1 pound lump crabmeat

1 cup heavy cream

4 tablespoons finely chopped chives

1 In a 2-quart saucepan over medium heat, add butter. Once butter has melted and foams, add onion and celery. Sauté 5 minutes or until very tender. Add garlic and cook 30 seconds.

2 Sprinkle flour over vegetables and cook, stirring constantly, 2 minutes. Reduce heat to low and whisk in wine. Once fully combined, whisk in seafood stock until also thoroughly combined.

3 Increase heat to medium-high and bring mixture to a boil while stirring constantly, then reduce heat to medium-low and simmer 5 minutes.

4 Turn off heat and purée soup with an immersion blender until smooth or, working in batches, purée soup in a blender and return to pan.

5 Heat pan over low heat and add crabmeat and cream. Stir well until soup is steaming, about 3 minutes. Serve hot with chives for garnish.

Wendy's Apple Pecan Salad

SERVES 2

WENDY'S PICK-UP WINDOW

Founded by Dave Thomas in 1969, Wendy's was popular for their square all-beef patties. Did you know they pioneered the modern drive-through? They called it the "Pick-Up Window" and had to teach customers how to use the order speaker system!

From 1979 to the mid-2000s, Wendy's had self-serve salad bars in their restaurants. Today they offer more upscale flavors like this salad made with crisp apples, creamy blue cheese, and toasty pecans.

Dressing

¼ cup pomegranate juice

¼ cup orange juice

2 tablespoons extra-virgin olive oil

1 tablespoon white wine vinegar

1 tablespoon granulated sugar

1 teaspoon Dijon mustard

¼ teaspoon onion powder

¼ teaspoon salt

¼ teaspoon ground black pepper

Salad

6 cups chopped romaine lettuce

3 cups spring mix

2 cups chopped grilled chicken breast strips

1 cup diced Fuji apple

½ cup dried cranberries

½ cup candied pecans

½ cup crumbled blue cheese

1 For the dressing: In a pint jar with a lid, add all ingredients. Cover and shake 30 seconds. Set aside.

2 For the salad: In a large bowl, combine romaine and spring mix and toss to combine. Add remaining ingredients and toss to mix. Divide salad between serving plates. Drizzle with dressing. Serve immediately.

CHAPTER 5

Sandwiches and Burgers

Arby's Classic Roast Beef Sandwiches

SERVES 4

Arby's restaurants have been around serving roast beef sandwiches since 1964. They did not offer additional menu items until the 1970s when the chain began to expand. Their roast beef sandwich remains one of the chain's most popular and iconic selections.

Sauce

1 cup ketchup

2 teaspoons water

2 teaspoons packed light brown sugar

½ teaspoon Worcestershire sauce

½ teaspoon Tabasco sauce

¼ teaspoon onion powder

¼ teaspoon garlic powder

¼ teaspoon salt

¼ teaspoon ground black pepper

Sandwiches

1 pound thinly sliced deli roast beef

1 (14.5-ounce) can beef broth

1 tablespoon salted butter, melted

4 plain hamburger buns, sliced in half lengthwise

1 For the sauce: Combine all ingredients in a small saucepan over medium heat. Stir constantly until sauce boils, about 5 minutes. Cook 7–10 minutes until sauce coats back of spoon thickly. Remove from heat and allow to cool.

2 For the sandwiches: Place roast beef and broth in a medium microwave-safe bowl. Heat 1–2 minutes until warm. Add a light coating of butter to both halves of each bun and toast cut sides of bun lightly in a 10-inch skillet over medium heat.

3 Place warm roast beef on bottom half of each bun, top with sauce, and cover with top half of bun. Serve.

Carl's Jr. Big Angus Famous Star

If you are looking for a big sit-down-restaurant-style burger on the go, the Big Angus Famous Star is for you! This copycat version has all the flavor without the trip to the drive-through.

SERVES 1

½ pound 80/20 ground Angus beef

¼ teaspoon salt

¼ teaspoon ground black pepper

1 (5-inch) hamburger bun, sliced in half lengthwise

3 teaspoons mayonnaise

2 teaspoons ketchup

1 teaspoon mustard

4 dill pickle slices

1 leaf iceberg lettuce

2 (¼-inch) slices beefsteak tomato

4 (⅛-inch) slices red onion rings

1 slice American cheese

BIG BURGERS AT CARL'S JR.

Carl's Jr. is well known for selling big sit-down-restaurant-style burgers! They started with the Six Dollar Burger, but with inflation the price rose and they renamed it the Thickburger. These days their big restaurant-style burger is the Big Angus Famous Star.

1 Preheat barbecue or smokeless indoor grill to medium heat.

2 Form ground beef into a 6-inch patty. Season both sides of patty with salt and pepper.

3 Grill patty 3–4 minutes per side until patty reaches an internal temperature of 145°F for medium, 155°F for medium-well, or 165°F for well-done.

4 Toast cut sides of bun in a 10-inch skillet over medium heat, about 3–4 minutes. Once toasted, spread mayonnaise on both halves of bun. Spread ketchup and mustard on top half of bun.

5 Arrange pickle slices on bottom half of bun. Add lettuce, tomato, and onion on top of pickles. Add burger and top with cheese and top half of bun. Serve immediately.

Carl's Jr. Single Western Bacon Cheeseburger

SERVES 1

This recipe provides all the classic ingredients in a western-style hamburger served at many restaurants but without the big price tag. Add some French fries and you have a fast-food meal at home.

2 frozen onion rings

¼ pound 80/20 ground beef

2 strips thick-cut smoked bacon

1 sesame seed hamburger bun, sliced in half lengthwise

2 tablespoons barbecue sauce

1 slice American cheese

1 Bake onion rings according to package directions.
2 Preheat barbecue or smokeless indoor grill to medium heat.
3 Form ground beef into a ½-inch-thick patty and cook 4–5 minutes per side until patty reaches an internal temperature of 145°F for medium, 155°F for medium-well, or 165°F for well-done.
4 In a 10-inch skillet over medium heat, fry bacon until crispy, about 8 minutes. Transfer to a paper towel-lined plate to drain.
5 Clean out skillet and return to medium heat. Add bun halves to pan, cut sides down, and toast, about 3 minutes.
6 Spread barbecue sauce on both halves of bun. Place onion rings on bottom half of bun. Add burger, cheese, bacon, and top half of bun. Serve immediately.

Chick-fil-A Chicken Sandwiches

Chick-fil-A is the largest chicken sandwich chain in America. Their original chicken sandwich is famous for its simplicity: toasted bun, fried chicken breast fillet, and dill pickles. It is a classic for a reason!

SERVES 2

2 (6-ounce) boneless, skinless chicken breast fillets

¼ cup low-fat buttermilk

2 tablespoons dill pickle brine

1 teaspoon granulated sugar

Vegetable oil, for frying

½ cup all-purpose flour

1 teaspoon ground black pepper

½ teaspoon salt

½ teaspoon paprika

1 tablespoon salted butter

2 plain hamburger buns, sliced in half lengthwise

6 dill pickle slices

1 In a large resealable plastic bag, add chicken, buttermilk, pickle brine, and sugar. Seal bag, removing as much air as you can, and massage to evenly coat chicken and combine marinade ingredients. Refrigerate at least 2 hours or up to 24 hours.

2 Remove chicken from refrigerator 30 minutes before cooking to warm to room temperature.

3 Fill deep fryer with oil per manufacturer directions and heat to 350°F, or in a 5½-quart Dutch oven add enough oil to fill pot by 3 inches, leaving at least 3 inches of space at the top, and place over medium-high heat until oil reaches 350°F.

4 In a medium bowl, add flour, pepper, salt, and paprika and mix well to combine. Remove chicken from marinade and let excess drip off. Dredge chicken in flour mixture, shaking off excess flour, and gently place in hot oil. Fry 5–7 minutes until chicken reaches an internal temperature of 165°F. Remove chicken from oil and let drain on a paper towel–lined plate.

5 Heat a 10-inch skillet over medium heat. Once hot, add butter and swirl to coat pan evenly. Add bun halves cut side down and toast until golden, about 3 minutes, swirling bun halves around pan to absorb all melted butter.

6 Place bottom half of each bun on a serving plate. Top with 3 pickle slices and 1 chicken breast each. Top with top bun. Serve immediately.

CHICK-FIL-A CHICKEN SANDWICHES

Chick-fil-A Grilled Chicken Club Sandwiches

The Grilled Chicken Club Sandwich was introduced in 1993 as part of Chick-fil-A's offerings for health-conscious customers. The chicken is marinated, like the fried version, in a seasoned marinade that includes pickle juice so it has a similar flavor.

SERVES 2

2 (6-ounce) boneless, skinless chicken breast fillets

¼ cup low-fat buttermilk

2 tablespoons dill pickle brine

1 teaspoon granulated sugar

1 teaspoon ground black pepper

½ teaspoon salt

½ teaspoon paprika

1 tablespoon salted butter

2 multigrain hamburger buns, sliced in half lengthwise

2 tablespoons honey mustard dressing

1 tablespoon barbecue sauce

2 green leaf lettuce leaves

4 (¼-inch) slices beefsteak tomato

2 slices Colby jack cheese

4 strips thick-cut bacon, cooked crisp

CHICK-FIL-A ON SUNDAY

Chick-fil-A restaurants are famous for being closed on Sundays so their employees can spend time with family or worship if they choose. This makes their most ardent fans very sad if a craving for their popular menu offerings hits, so much so that there are many Internet memes of sad people unable to get a chicken sandwich!

1 In a large resealable plastic bag, add chicken, buttermilk, pickle brine, sugar, pepper, salt, and paprika. Seal bag, removing as much air as you can, and massage to evenly coat chicken and combine marinade ingredients. Refrigerate at least 2 hours or up to 24 hours.

2 Preheat barbecue or smokeless indoor grill to medium heat.

3 Remove chicken from marinade and let excess drain off. Grill chicken 3–4 minutes per side until chicken reaches an internal temperature of 165°F.

4 Heat a 10-inch skillet over medium heat. Once hot, add butter and swirl to coat pan evenly. Add bun halves cut side down and toast until golden, about 3 minutes, swirling bun halves around pan to absorb all melted butter.

5 In a small bowl, add honey mustard dressing and barbecue sauce. Mix until well combined.

6 Place bottom half of each bun on a serving plate and spread with half of prepared sauce. Top with 1 lettuce leaf, 2 tomato slices, 1 chicken breast, 1 cheese slice, and 2 strips bacon each. Top with top half of bun. Serve immediately.

Hardee's Mushroom & Swiss

SERVES 4

Hardee's charbroils their burgers, giving them a smoky grilled flavor. For the most authentic flavor at home, grilling your burgers on an outdoor grill will add a flavor similar to the restaurant's.

1 (10.75-ounce) can Campbell's Golden Mushroom Soup

1 cup sliced button mushrooms

1 teaspoon Worcestershire sauce

½ teaspoon Accent Flavor Enhancer

½ teaspoon Lawry's Seasoned Salt

¼ teaspoon ground black pepper

1 pound 80/20 ground beef

4 plain hamburger buns, sliced in half lengthwise

4 slices Swiss cheese

1 In a medium bowl, mix together mushroom soup, mushrooms, and Worcestershire sauce. Place mixture in a 1-quart saucepan over low heat and bring to a simmer, about 5 minutes. Stir and simmer 5 minutes or until mushrooms are tender. Remove from heat and cover to keep warm.

2 In a medium bowl, add Accent Flavor Enhancer, Lawry's Seasoned Salt, and pepper. Mix well. Add ground beef and gently mix to combine. Form mixture into four (½-inch-thick) patties.

3 Preheat barbecue or smokeless indoor grill to medium heat.

4 Grill patties 4–5 minutes per side until patties reach an internal temperature of 145°F for medium, 155°F for medium-well, or 165°F for well-done.

5 Place each patty on bottom half of a bun, add 1 slice Swiss cheese each, and top with mushroom sauce and top half of bun. Serve immediately.

In-N-Out Burger Double-Double

"Double-Double" is short for "double meat, double cheese" and is what most people think of when they think In-N-Out. To make this burger "Animal Style," brush both sides of patty with 1/4 teaspoon yellow mustard before grilling.

1 plain hamburger bun, sliced in half lengthwise

1/3 pound 80/20 ground beef

2 slices American cheese

1 tablespoon Thousand Island dressing

1 (1/4-inch) slice beefsteak tomato

1 leaf iceberg lettuce

1 (1/8-inch) slice yellow onion

1 Heat a 10-inch skillet over medium heat. Add bun halves cut side down and toast until golden, about 3 minutes. Set aside.

2 Form ground beef into two (1/4-inch-thick) patties. Season patties with salt and pepper. Cook 4–5 minutes per side until patties reach an internal temperature of 165°F for well-done. In the last 30 seconds of cooking, place 1 slice cheese on each patty and melt cheese.

3 Place bottom half of bun on a serving plate and spread with salad dressing. Top with tomato, lettuce, burger patty, onion, burger patty, and top half of bun. Serve immediately.

SERVES 1

IN-N-OUT

The In-N-Out Burger restaurant chain has developed an almost cult following for its hamburgers in the western states and is growing across America, winning new fans if the long lines at the drive-through are any indication!

Jack in the Box Sourdough Jack

SERVES 1

Introduced as the Sourdough Jack in 1997, this burger was originally added to the menu in 1989 and called the "Grilled Sourdough Burger." It was intended to be a more sophisticated burger for adults.

¼ pound 80/20 ground beef

¼ teaspoon salt

¼ teaspoon ground black pepper

2 strips thick-cut smoked bacon

1 tablespoon salted butter

2 slices sourdough bread

2 tablespoons mayonnaise

1 tablespoon ketchup

1 slice Swiss cheese

1 (¼-inch) slice beefsteak tomato

1 Preheat barbecue or smokeless indoor grill to medium heat.

2 Form ground beef into a ¼-inch-thick patty and season both sides with salt and pepper. Cook 4–5 minutes per side until patty reaches an internal temperature of 165°F for well-done.

3 In a 10-inch skillet over medium heat, fry bacon until crispy, about 8 minutes. Transfer to a paper towel-lined plate to drain.

4 Clean out skillet and return to medium heat. Add butter and once melted, add sourdough bread and toast until golden brown, about 3 minutes.

5 Place 1 slice sourdough bread toasted side down on a serving plate. Spread with mayonnaise and ketchup. Top with burger patty, cheese, tomato, bacon, and second bread slice toasted side up. Serve immediately.

Jersey Mike's Club Sub

When ordering a sub from Jersey Mike's, you can customize the toppings to your preference. One popular option is to order it "Mikes Way," with onion, lettuce, tomato, olive oil, red wine vinegar, and spices.

SERVES 1

1 (6-inch) sub roll, sliced in half lengthwise

2 slices provolone cheese

2 ounces thin-sliced deli ham

2 ounces thin-sliced deli turkey

½ cup shredded iceberg lettuce

¼ cup thin-sliced yellow onion

3 (⅛-inch) slices beefsteak tomato

2 teaspoons extra-virgin olive oil

2 teaspoons red wine vinegar

¼ teaspoon dried oregano

2 strips thick-cut smoked bacon, cooked crisp

1 tablespoon mayonnaise

1 Place sub roll on a serving plate. On bottom half of roll, layer cheese, ham, turkey, lettuce, onion, and tomato. Drizzle olive oil and vinegar over top, sprinkle with oregano, and top with bacon.

2 Spread top half of roll with mayonnaise and add to sandwich. Serve immediately.

Jersey Mike's The Original Italian

SERVES 1

You can find all the deli meats for this sandwich in your grocery store's deli department. You can also make this a "sub in a tub" by eliminating the roll, rolling the meats and cheeses, and slicing and layering them with the remaining ingredients over 2 cups shredded lettuce.

1 (6-inch) sub roll, sliced in half lengthwise

2 slices provolone cheese

1 ounce thin-sliced deli ham

½ ounce thin-sliced prosciuttini

½ ounce thin-sliced hot capicola

½ ounce thin-sliced hard salami

½ ounce thin-sliced sandwich pepperoni

½ cup shredded iceberg lettuce

¼ cup thin-sliced yellow onion

3 (⅛-inch) slices beefsteak tomato

2 teaspoons extra-virgin olive oil

2 teaspoons red wine vinegar

¼ teaspoon dried oregano

1 Place sub roll on a serving plate. On bottom half of roll, layer cheese, ham, prosciuttini, capicola, salami, pepperoni, lettuce, onion, and tomato.

2 Drizzle olive oil and vinegar over top and sprinkle with oregano. Top with top half of roll and enjoy.

JERSEY MIKE'S THE ORIGINAL ITALIAN

McDonald's Filet-O-Fish

FILET-O-FISH

The Filet-O-Fish was created by McDonald's in 1963. It is a very easy sandwich to make using frozen fish from Gorton's, which supplied the fish to all the restaurants when the concept was developed.

This recipe tastes better than the original and contains less fat since the fish is baked instead of fried.

1 Gorton's Crunchy Breaded Fish Fillet

1 plain hamburger bun, sliced in half lengthwise

1 tablespoon mayonnaise

1 teaspoon minced yellow onion

1 teaspoon sweet relish

$1/16$ teaspoon salt

1 slice American cheese

1 Cook fish according to package instructions.
2 On a 10-inch skillet over medium heat, add bun halves cut side down. Lightly grill bun halves until toasted, about 3 minutes. Set aside.
3 In a small bowl, mix together mayonnaise, onion, relish, and salt to make tartar sauce.
4 Place fish on bottom half of bun. Top with cheese, tartar sauce, and top half of bun. Serve immediately.

Panera Bread Chipotle Chicken Avocado Melt

Panera is famous for their deli sandwiches, and this one is among their most popular.

1 (5-inch) focaccia bread square, sliced in half lengthwise

1 tablespoon chipotle mayonnaise

2 slices smoked Gouda cheese

$1/2$ cup shredded smoked chicken breast

1 teaspoon finely chopped fresh cilantro

$1/4$ cup chopped peppadew peppers

$1/2$ medium avocado, thinly sliced

1 Preheat oven to 350°F and line a quarter sheet pan with parchment.
2 Place focaccia bread on prepared sheet pan cut side up and spread top half with mayonnaise. Top each half with cheese. Add chicken to bottom half and spread evenly.
3 Bake 5 minutes or until cheese is melted. Remove from oven and add cilantro, peppadew peppers, and avocado. Top with top half of bread. Serve hot.

Popeyes Chicken Sandwiches

If you prefer the spicy version of the viral Popeyes Chicken Sandwich, simply add 1 teaspoon hot sauce and 1/8 teaspoon cayenne pepper to the mayonnaise and stir well.

2 (4-ounce) boneless, skinless chicken breasts

2/3 cup low-fat buttermilk, divided

1 tablespoon Cajun seasoning, divided

1 cup all-purpose flour

1/3 cup cornstarch

Vegetable oil, for frying

2 brioche hamburger buns, sliced in half lengthwise

1/4 cup mayonnaise

6 thick-cut dill pickle slices

THE VIRAL CHICKEN SANDWICH

In 2019, Popeyes debuted their Chicken Sandwich, which, thanks to the power of social media, quickly went viral. Everyone wanted to see if it was worth the hype, and some locations went from selling about sixty sandwiches a day to as many as 1,000!

1 In a large resealable plastic bag, combine chicken, 1/3 cup buttermilk, and 1 teaspoon Cajun seasoning. Seal bag and massage until chicken is evenly coated. Refrigerate 2 hours or overnight.

2 In a medium bowl, combine flour, cornstarch, and remaining Cajun seasoning. Whisk well to combine. In a 6-inch dish, add remaining buttermilk. Set aside.

3 Once chicken has marinated, remove from bag and let excess marinade drip off. Add chicken to flour mixture and turn to coat. Tap off excess flour and add to buttermilk, turning to coat. Let excess buttermilk drip off and return chicken to flour mixture and coat evenly on all sides. Place coated chicken on a wire rack over a quarter sheet pan and let stand at room temperature to let coating dry and allow chicken to warm slightly while you heat oil.

4 Fill deep fryer with oil per manufacturer directions and heat to 350°F, or in a 5½-quart Dutch oven add enough oil to fill pot by 3 inches, leaving at least 3 inches of space at the top, and place over medium-high heat until oil reaches 350°F.

5 Add chicken to hot oil. Fry 4–5 minutes per side until chicken is golden brown and reaches an internal temperature of 165°F.

6 Transfer chicken to a paper towel–lined plate.

7 Spread both halves of each bun with mayonnaise. Place 1 chicken breast on bottom half of each bun, top each with 3 pickle slices, then add top half of bun and enjoy immediately.

Quiznos French Dip

Quiznos has a variety of toasted deli sandwiches. This recipe features one of their signature submarines.

PRESSED SANDWICHES

You can transform any sandwich you want into a panini using either a folding grill, such as a George Forman grill or two cast iron skillets. For the grill, place sandwich inside preheated grill and place a heavy pot on top of grill to press sandwich, about 3–5 minutes. With cast iron skillets, heat both over medium heat for 5 minutes. Remove from heat. Add sandwich inside one skillet, top with foil, and place second skillet on top bottom side down. Toast until golden, about 3–5 minutes.

Au Jus Dipping Sauce

1 tablespoon salted butter

1 tablespoon finely chopped yellow onion

1 tablespoon all-purpose flour

1 (1-ounce) packet au jus mix

1⅔ cups water

Sandwich Sauce

½ cup Alfredo sauce

¼ cup mayonnaise

⅛ teaspoon onion salt or garlic salt

Sandwiches

1 loaf bakery French bread

¾ pound thin-sliced deli roast beef

½ cup shredded Swiss cheese

½ cup shredded Italian cheese blend

1 Preheat oven broiler to 500°F.

2 For the au jus dipping sauce: Melt butter in a small saucepan over medium heat. Add onion and sauté until tender, about 2–3 minutes.

3 Add flour and contents of au jus mix packet. Gradually whisk in water and allow to simmer while you make the sandwich and sauce.

4 For the sandwich sauce: In a small bowl, mix together Alfredo sauce, mayonnaise, and onion salt.

5 For the sandwiches: Slice French bread with a single horizontal slice to make a top and a bottom half. Spread sauce evenly over both halves.

6 Place bread halves open-faced on an ungreased quarter baking sheet. Place under oven broiler 1 minute or until sauce is bubbly and edges of bread barely start to brown.

7 Remove baking sheet from oven. Divide roast beef evenly between bread halves, then sprinkle evenly with cheeses.

8 Broil 1 minute more or until cheeses melt and start to brown. Remove from oven.

9 Place top sandwich half over bottom half and return to broiler for 1–2 minutes to lightly toast top of sandwich. Remove from oven and slice sandwich into four even slices.

10 Serve with au jus sauce in small bowls for dipping.

Red Robin Banzai

Fresh pineapple slices can be found in most grocery store produce departments, and when in season from March to July, pineapple has the best flavor. If you can't find fresh pineapple, feel free to substitute with canned rings in juice.

¼ pound 80/20 ground beef

¼ teaspoon salt

¼ teaspoon ground black pepper

¼ teaspoon onion powder

⅛ teaspoon garlic powder

⅛ teaspoon granulated sugar

⅛ teaspoon paprika

1 tablespoon teriyaki sauce

1 fresh pineapple ring

1 tablespoon salted butter

1 plain hamburger bun, sliced in half lengthwise

2 tablespoons mayonnaise

1 slice Cheddar cheese

2 (⅛-inch) slices beefsteak tomato

¼ cup shredded iceberg lettuce

1 Preheat barbecue or smokeless indoor grill to medium heat.

2 Form ground beef into a ¼-inch-thick patty and season both sides with salt, pepper, onion powder, garlic powder, sugar, and paprika. Cook 4–5 minutes per side until patty reaches an internal temperature of 165°F for well-done. Remove patty from grill and brush with teriyaki sauce.

3 To heated grill, add pineapple ring and cook 2 minutes per side or until pineapple is lightly charred and tender. Set aside.

4 Heat a 10-inch skillet over medium heat. Add butter and once melted, add bun halves cut side down and toast until golden brown, about 3 minutes.

5 Place bottom half of bun on a serving plate. Spread with mayonnaise. Top with burger patty, cheese, pineapple, tomato, and lettuce. Top with top half of bun. Serve immediately.

Red Robin Royal Red Robin Burger

SERVES 1

Red Robin was founded in 1969, and today they have more than five hundred locations in the US and Canada. The restaurant is famous for their gourmet burgers, and the Royal Red Robin Burger has been a menu staple since they first opened.

¼ pound 80/20 ground beef

¼ teaspoon salt

¼ teaspoon ground black pepper

¼ teaspoon onion powder

⅛ teaspoon garlic powder

⅛ teaspoon granulated sugar

⅛ teaspoon paprika

2 strips thick-cut smoked bacon

1 large egg

1 tablespoon salted butter

1 plain hamburger bun, sliced in half lengthwise

2 tablespoons mayonnaise

¼ cup shredded iceberg lettuce

2 (½-inch) slices beefsteak tomato

2 slices American cheese

1 Preheat barbecue or smokeless indoor grill to medium heat.

2 Form ground beef into a ¼-inch-thick patty and season both sides with salt, pepper, onion powder, garlic powder, sugar, and paprika. Cook 4–5 minutes per side until patty reaches an internal temperature of 165°F for well-done.

3 In a 10-inch skillet over medium heat, fry bacon until crispy, about 8 minutes. Remove bacon from pan and transfer to a paper towel–lined plate to cool.

4 To same skillet over medium heat, add egg. Fry 2–2½ minutes until white is fully set but yolk is still soft. Transfer to plate with bacon and set aside.

5 Clean out skillet and return to medium heat. Add butter and once melted, add bun halves cut side down and toast until golden brown, about 3 minutes.

6 Place bottom half of bun on a serving plate. Spread with mayonnaise. Top with lettuce, tomato, burger patty, cheese, bacon, and egg. Top with top half of bun. Serve immediately.

Red Robin Whiskey River BBQ

Red Robin sells their popular Whiskey River BBQ Sauce, as well as their Original Blend Signature Seasoning, online and in select retail stores if you want to have the most authentic restaurant flavor at home.

SERVES 1

¼ large sweet onion, thinly sliced

¼ cup low-fat buttermilk

½ cup all-purpose flour

¼ teaspoon seasoning salt

1 cup vegetable oil

¼ pound 80/20 ground beef

¼ teaspoon salt

¼ teaspoon ground black pepper

¼ teaspoon onion powder

⅛ teaspoon garlic powder

⅛ teaspoon granulated sugar

⅛ teaspoon paprika

1 tablespoon salted butter

1 plain hamburger bun, sliced in half lengthwise

2 tablespoons mayonnaise

1 tablespoon barbecue sauce

1 slice Cheddar cheese

2 (⅛-inch) slices beefsteak tomato

¼ cup shredded iceberg lettuce

1 In a medium bowl, add onion and buttermilk. Toss to coat onion, then cover and let soak 30 minutes.

2 While onion soaks, combine flour and seasoning salt in a resealable plastic bag and shake to combine.

3 Once soaked, drain excess buttermilk from onion. Place onion in bag with flour, seal, and shake well to coat.

4 Fill 2-quart saucepan with oil over high heat and heat to 350°F.

5 Add onion and cook 2–3 minutes, turning occasionally, until golden brown and tender. Transfer to a paper towel lined–plate and set aside.

6 Preheat barbecue or smokeless indoor grill to medium heat.

7 Form ground beef into a ¼-inch-thick patty and season both sides with salt, pepper, onion powder, garlic powder, sugar, and paprika. Cook 4–5 minutes per side until patty reaches an internal temperature of 165°F for well-done.

8 Heat a 10-inch skillet over medium heat. Add butter and once melted, add bun halves cut side down and toast 3 minutes.

9 Place bottom half of bun on a serving plate. Spread with mayonnaise. Top with fried onion, burger patty, barbecue sauce, cheese, tomato, and lettuce. Top with top half of bun. Serve immediately.

RED ROBIN WHISKEY RIVER BBQ

Sonic Fritos Chili Cheese Wraps

The Sonic Fritos Chili Cheese Wrap is a popular limited-time menu offering that is usually part of their special summer menu. With this recipe you can enjoy it year-round.

SERVES 4

1 (19-ounce) can mild beef chili

3 cups Fritos corn chips

4 (8-inch) flour tortillas

1 cup shredded mild Cheddar cheese

¼ cup diced green onions

1 In a small saucepan, cook chili over medium-high heat until bubbling. Remove from stove and fold in Fritos.

2 Place a fourth of the chili mixture down the middle of each tortilla. Sprinkle ¼ cup cheese on top of chili. Add green onions. Fold tortilla into a burrito.

3 Microwave 15–20 seconds to melt cheese. Serve.

Sonic Hickory BBQ Cheeseburger

SERVES 1

Founded in 1953 in Oklahoma as the Top Hat Drive-In, today Sonic is the best-known drive-in fast-food burger brand in America. They are best known for burgers, specialty drinks, and ice cream treats.

¼ pound 80/20 ground beef

¼ teaspoon salt

¼ teaspoon ground black pepper

1 tablespoon salted butter

1 large plain hamburger bun, sliced in half lengthwise

1 slice American cheese

1 tablespoon chopped white onion

⅓ cup chopped lettuce

3 dill pickle slices

1 tablespoon mayonnaise

1 tablespoon Kraft Hickory Smoke Barbecue Sauce

1 Preheat a 10-inch skillet over medium heat.

2 Shape ground beef into a ¼-inch patty. Season both sides with salt and pepper. Set aside.

3 Add butter to skillet and once melted, add bun halves cut side down and toast until golden brown, about 3 minutes. Remove from skillet and set aside.

4 In same skillet over medium heat, add burger patty. Cook 3–4 minutes per side until patty reaches an internal temperature of 165°F for well-done.

5 Place bottom half of bun on a serving plate. Add cheese to bun and top with burger patty, onion, lettuce, and pickle slices. Spread top half of bun with mayonnaise and barbecue sauce and place on top of pickle slices. Serve immediately.

Subway Sweet Onion Chicken Teriyaki

Subway's Sweet Onion Chicken Teriyaki is one of the chain's biggest-selling subs. This sub is made with very common ingredients; what sets it apart is the sweet onion sauce.

SERVES 1

1 (4-ounce) boneless, skinless chicken breast

¼ cup Lawry's Teriyaki Marinade

½ cup light corn syrup

1 tablespoon red wine vinegar

1 tablespoon minced white onion

2 tablespoons white vinegar

1 teaspoon packed light brown sugar

1 teaspoon balsamic vinegar

¼ teaspoon lemon juice

⅛ teaspoon salt

⅛ teaspoon poppy seeds

⅛ teaspoon ground black pepper

⅛ teaspoon garlic powder

½ cup shredded iceberg lettuce

3 (⅛-inch) slices beefsteak tomato

⅛ cup thinly sliced red onion

1 (6-inch) white sub roll, sliced lengthwise

1 Place chicken breast and marinade in a large resealable plastic bag. Marinate chicken in refrigerator at least 30 minutes or up to 4 hours.

2 Combine corn syrup, red wine vinegar, white onion, white vinegar, brown sugar, balsamic vinegar, lemon juice, salt, poppy seeds, pepper, and garlic powder in a 1-quart saucepan. Heat over medium heat until mixture comes to a boil, about 5 minutes. Remove from heat, stir well, cover, and let cool.

3 Preheat barbecue or smokeless indoor grill to medium heat.

4 Cook chicken 4–5 minutes per side until it reaches an internal temperature of 165°F. Remove from grill and cool 3 minutes before slicing into ¼-inch strips.

5 Place lettuce, tomato, and red onion on bottom half of sub roll. Add chicken and drizzle with prepared sauce. Top with top half of sub roll. Serve immediately.

Subway Tuna

SERVES 1

This simple tuna salad is perfect for sandwiches, salads, or enjoying with crackers as a snack.

1 (5-ounce) can tuna packed in oil, drained

2 tablespoons mayonnaise

1 teaspoon lemon juice

1 (6-inch) whole-wheat sub roll, sliced in half lengthwise

½ cup shredded iceberg lettuce

⅛ cup thinly sliced red onion

6 dill pickle slices

1 In a medium bowl, add tuna, mayonnaise, and lemon juice. With a fork, blend the mixture making sure to break up chunks of tuna until smooth.

2 Spread tuna mixture on sub roll. Top with lettuce, onion, and pickle slices. Serve immediately.

Subway Veggie Delite Sandwich on Flatbread

SERVES 1

This light and low-calorie option on the menu at Subway is easy to create at home using simple ingredients. You can customize this sandwich with your favorite vegetables or omit the ones you don't like.

1 (6-inch) flatbread

1 slice pepper jack cheese

½ cup shredded lettuce

¼ cup thinly sliced English cucumber

3 (⅛-inch) slices beefsteak tomato

¼ cup sliced green bell pepper

⅛ cup thinly sliced red onion

4 dill pickle slices

5 sliced black olives

1 tablespoon Italian salad dressing

1 Place flatbread on a medium microwave-safe plate and top with cheese. Heat 30 seconds or until cheese melts.

2 Top cheese with lettuce, cucumber, tomato, pepper, onion, pickle slices, and olives. Drizzle salad dressing over top vegetables. Fold sandwich in half and enjoy immediately.

Wendy's Spicy Chicken Sandwiches

These super-crispy chicken sandwiches with a hint of spiciness will feed your fast-food craving. If you like it really hot, add more hot pepper sauce to your taste.

SERVES 4

Vegetable oil, for frying

1/3 cup hot pepper sauce

2/3 cup water

3/4 cup all-purpose flour

1/4 cup cornstarch

2 1/2 teaspoons salt

4 teaspoons cayenne pepper

1 teaspoon ground black pepper

1 teaspoon onion powder

1/2 teaspoon paprika

1/8 teaspoon garlic powder

4 (5-ounce) boneless, skinless chicken breasts

4 plain hamburger buns, sliced in half lengthwise

4 tablespoons mayonnaise

4 (1/4-inch) slices beefsteak tomato

4 green leaf lettuce leaves

1 Fill deep fryer with oil per manufacturer directions and heat to 350°F, or in a 5½-quart Dutch oven add enough oil to fill pot by 3 inches, leaving at least 3 inches of space at the top, and place over medium-high heat until oil reaches 350°F.

2 In a small bowl, mix hot pepper sauce and water.

3 In a medium bowl, combine flour, cornstarch, salt, cayenne pepper, black pepper, onion powder, paprika, and garlic powder.

4 Pound each chicken breast to ⅜-inch thickness. Trim if necessary to fit on bun half.

5 Coat 1 chicken breast with flour mixture and then place in watered-down pepper sauce, turning to coat. Lift from sauce and let excess drip off, then coat in flour mixture again and set aside. Repeat with remaining chicken.

6 Fry chicken in hot oil 10 minutes or until brown and crispy. Remove to paper towels to drain.

7 Cook hamburger bun halves cut side down in a hot fry pan. Spread 2 teaspoons mayonnaise on both halves of each bun.

8 Add 1 tomato, 1 leaf lettuce, and 1 chicken breast to bottom half of each bun. Top with top half of bun. Serve immediately.

White Castle Original Sliders

SERVES 6 (YIELDS 24 SLIDER SANDWICHES)

ORIGINS OF THE SLIDER

The oldest fast-food chain in the country, White Castle lays claim to inventing the slider. They used the term "slider" to describe their little square hamburger patties. White Castle burgers sold for a nickel a piece in the 1920s and still have a cultlike following to this day.

White Castile is a popular Midwest burger chain famous for their sliders. The sliders' famous flavor comes from the onion cooked with the burger patties. This version makes cooking the patties easier while keeping the original flavor.

¼ **cup dried minced onions**

¾ **cup hot water**

2 **pounds 80/20 ground beef**

½ **teaspoon salt**

2 **(24-count) packages King's Hawaiian Savory Butter Rolls**

1 Preheat oven to 350°F.

2 In a medium bowl, add dry onions and hot water. Let onions soak 20 minutes. Drain well.

3 In a large mixing bowl, combine ground beef, salt, and rehydrated onion. Mix until just combined. Divide mixture evenly between two ungreased half sheet pans. Spread beef into a ⅛-inch-thick rectangle.

4 Bake 20 minutes. Drain excess oil from pans, then cut beef into twenty-four squares with a pizza cutter.

5 Slice Hawaiian rolls into individual rolls and then slice each roll in half. Place roll halves in microwave and heat 20 seconds to soften. Place a beef patty on bottom half of each roll and top with top half. Serve hot.

CHAPTER 6

Beef, Chicken, and Pork Entrées

Applebee's Bourbon Street Steaks

SERVES 4

This Cajun-style dish is named after the famous street in the French Quarter in New Orleans. Serve these steaks with mashed potatoes and sautéed mushrooms and onions for the full restaurant experience.

½ cup bottled steak sauce

¼ cup bourbon whiskey

1 tablespoon honey

2 teaspoons prepared mustard

4 (8-ounce) USDA top sirloin select steaks

4 tablespoons garlic herb butter, such as Kerrygold

1 In a large resealable plastic bag, combine steak sauce, whiskey, honey, and mustard. Add steaks, remove air from bag, and seal. Massage lightly to cover steaks. Refrigerate 2 hours or overnight.

2 Preheat outdoor barbecue or smokeless indoor grill to medium-high heat.

3 Grill steaks 4 minutes per side for rare, 5 minutes per side for medium, or 7 minutes per side for well-done. Remove steaks from grill to serving plates and top each with garlic herb butter. Serve hot.

Applebee's Double-Glazed Baby Back Ribs

Applebee's was founded in 1980 as a neighborhood pub that served good-quality food. These spicy, sweet, delicious glazed baby back ribs are among their famous entrées.

SERVES 6

3 racks pork baby back ribs

1 cup ketchup

¼ cup apple cider vinegar

3 tablespoons packed dark brown sugar

3 tablespoons Worcestershire sauce

1 teaspoon liquid smoke

½ teaspoon salt

1 Place ribs in an 8-quart stockpot with enough water to cover them. Bring water to a boil over high heat, reduce heat to medium-low, and cover. Simmer 1 hour or until ribs are fork-tender.

2 Mix remaining ingredients in a medium saucepan. Bring to a boil over medium heat, reduce heat to low, and simmer uncovered. Cook 30 minutes, stirring often, or until sauce is slightly thickened.

3 Heat broiler to 550°F. Place ribs meat side down on broiler pan. Brush ribs with half of prepared sauce.

4 Broil 4–5 inches from heat source 6–7 minutes. Turn ribs over and brush with remaining sauce.

5 Broil 6–7 minutes longer until edges are slightly charred. Serve.

APPLEBEE'S DOUBLE-GLAZED BABY BACK RIBS

Applebee's Fiesta Lime Chicken

The fiesta flavors in this chicken come from its margarita-inspired marinade. It is best not to marinate the chicken for this recipe more than 3 hours or the lime juice may make the chicken mushy.

SERVES 1

¼ cup lime juice

2 tablespoons tequila

1 (6-ounce) boneless, skinless chicken breast

1 tablespoon salsa

3 tablespoons ranch dressing

½ cup crushed tortilla chips

¼ cup shredded Cheddar jack cheese

1 lime wedge (⅙ of lime)

1 Pour lime juice and tequila into a large resealable plastic bag. Add chicken, remove air, seal, and allow to marinate 2–3 hours in refrigerator.

2 Preheat outdoor barbecue or indoor smokeless grill to medium-high heat and also preheat broiler to 500°F.

3 Remove chicken from marinade. Grill 4–5 minutes per side or until chicken reaches an internal temperature of 165°F. Remove from grill to a plate, tent with foil, and let rest.

4 Combine salsa and ranch dressing in a small bowl.

5 Scatter crushed tortilla chips on an oven-safe plate. Place chicken on top of crushed chips. Pour prepared dressing over chicken and top with cheese.

6 Place chicken under broiler until cheese is melted, about 3 minutes. Let cool 2 minutes before serving. Serve with lime wedge for spritzing over chicken.

Bob Evans Mushroom & Onion Chopped Steaks

SERVES 4

LEFTOVER CHOPPED STEAKS

If you find you have leftover chopped steaks, you can crumble them in a skillet with reserved sauce and vegetables and 1 tablespoon tomato paste per steak. Heat until steaming hot, about 3 minutes, then stir in 2–3 tablespoons water to loosen sauce. Spoon over fresh-cooked pasta for a quick beef pasta meal.

Founded as part of the popular breakfast sausage company, Bob Evans Restaurants have been open for over sixty years. They are famous for country-style comfort food and hearty breakfasts.

1 pound ground sirloin beef

½ teaspoon salt

½ teaspoon onion powder

¼ teaspoon ground black pepper

¼ teaspoon garlic powder

1 tablespoon vegetable oil

2 tablespoons salted butter

1 medium yellow onion, peeled and sliced

1 pound sliced button mushrooms

2 tablespoons all-purpose flour

2 cups beef stock

¼ cup heavy cream

1 In a medium bowl, combine ground beef, salt, onion powder, pepper, and garlic powder. Mix well, then form into 4 (1-inch-thick) patties.

2 In a 12-inch nonstick skillet over medium heat, add oil. Once hot, swirl to coat pan and add beef patties. Cook 3 minutes per side, then transfer to a plate.

3 To same skillet over medium heat, add butter. Once melted, add onion and mushrooms and sauté 4–5 minutes until tender.

4 Sprinkle flour over onion and mushrooms and cook 1 minute, then stir in beef stock, scraping bottom of pan to release any brown bits. Return patties to pan and bring mixture to a boil, about 2 minutes. Reduce heat to low, cover, and cook 10 minutes or until patties reach an internal temperature of 160°F.

5 Remove patties from skillet to serving plates. Increase heat under skillet to medium and stir sauce well. Bring to a boil and reduce sauce until thick enough to coat the back of a spoon. Stir in cream. Spoon sauce along with onion and mushrooms over steaks. Serve immediately.

Bob Evans Slow-Roasted Turkey

This savory herb-roasted turkey breast makes a delicious meal any time of year but is especially nice for the holiday season. Enjoy this with the Bob Evans Bread & Celery Dressing in Chapter 9.

SERVES 6

¼ cup salted butter

1 teaspoon poultry seasoning

½ teaspoon salt

½ teaspoon ground black pepper

¼ teaspoon ground sage

¼ teaspoon dried thyme

1 (3-pound) boneless, skinless turkey breast

1 In a medium bowl, mix together butter, poultry seasoning, salt, pepper, sage, and thyme. Spread over all sides of turkey breast. Place turkey in a 16-inch roasting pan and cover tightly with foil. Refrigerate 1 hour or overnight.

2 Preheat oven to 350°F.

3 Remove turkey from refrigerator 30 minutes before roasting. Once turkey has warmed up a little, place in the oven and roast 10 minutes with the foil on. Then remove foil and roast 75–80 minutes until center of turkey breast reaches 165°F.

4 Remove turkey from oven and loosely tent with foil. Let stand 15 minutes before slicing into ¼-inch-thick slices and serving.

Buca di Beppo Chicken Limone

SERVES 4

"Buca di Beppo" means "my buddy's basement," which explains the windowless dining rooms filled with eclectic decor. Opening in 1993, this chain is famous for their large portions, kitschy decor, and Pope rooms!

1 large egg

3 tablespoons lemon juice, divided

⅓ cup all-purpose flour

⅛ teaspoon garlic powder

⅛ teaspoon paprika

4 (6-ounce) boneless, skinless chicken breasts

¼ cup melted unsalted butter

2 teaspoons chicken bouillon paste, such as Better Than Bouillon

½ cup hot water

1 tablespoon capers

4 lemon wedges (⅙ lemon each)

1. In a small bowl, combine egg and 1 tablespoon lemon juice and beat well.
2. In a medium bowl, combine flour, garlic powder, and paprika and stir well.
3. Place chicken breasts between two sheets of wax paper and pound until chicken is flattened and even ½-inch in thickness.
4. Dip chicken in egg mixture, then dredge in flour mixture.
5. In a 10-inch skillet over medium-high heat, add butter and allow to melt. Cook chicken in butter 2–3 minutes on each side until browned.
6. In a small bowl, dissolve bouillon paste in hot water and add to chicken along with remaining lemon juice. Bring to a boil, cover, and reduce heat to medium-low.
7. Simmer 10–15 minutes until chicken reaches an internal temperature of at least 165°F. Garnish with capers and lemon wedges before serving.

Buca di Beppo Chicken Saltimbocca

The name "saltimbocca" means "jump into the mouth," because the dish is so delicious people will not be able to eat it fast enough! Serve with cooked pasta such as fettuccine or linguine or with mashed potatoes.

SERVES 4

1 teaspoon salt

4 (5-ounce) boneless, skinless chicken breasts

1 tablespoon chopped fresh sage

4 thin slices prosciutto

¼ cup olive oil

2 tablespoons all-purpose flour

4 ounces dry white wine

8 artichoke heart quarters

¼ cup fresh lemon juice

¼ heavy cream

1 tablespoon unsalted butter

1 tablespoon capers

1 Lightly salt chicken breasts and sprinkle evenly with sage. Place 1 slice prosciutto on top of each chicken breast. Lay a piece of wax paper over chicken and pound to ⅜-inch thickness.

2 In a 10-inch skillet over medium heat, add olive oil.

3 Add flour to a shallow dish and lightly dredge chicken in flour. Place chicken in pan, prosciutto side down. Cook 2 minutes or until lightly browned, then flip and cook second side 2–3 minutes until chicken reaches an internal temperature of 165°F. Remove chicken to a plate.

4 Drain off excess oil, then return pan to medium heat and deglaze pan with wine, scraping any brown bits from bottom of pan. Add artichoke, lemon juice, cream, and butter. Cook until butter is melted, about 30 seconds, then cook for 1 minute, stirring constantly. Return chicken to pan along with any juices on plate and turn to coat in sauce.

5 On a large platter, place chicken breasts, pour sauce from pan over chicken, and garnish with capers. Serve hot.

Burger King Chicken Fries

SERVES 2

Chicken Fries, introduced in 2005, are a fun item for both kids and adults on the Burger King menu. This restaurant copycat recipe is easy to make since it uses a prepared seasoning mix.

1 pound boneless, skinless chicken breasts

½ cup all-purpose flour

½ cup Zatarain's Regular Fish-Fri

1 large egg

1 tablespoon water

Vegetable oil, for frying

1 Cut chicken breasts in half lengthwise into cutlets. Cut each cutlet into ¼-inch-thick strips (shaped like French fries) with meat scissors or a knife.

2 Place flour and Fish-Fri in two separate large resealable plastic bags.

3 In a small bowl, lightly beat egg with water.

4 Place four chicken strips at a time into flour bag. Remove from bag and shake off excess flour. Dip in egg wash, shake off excess, then shake in Fish-Fri bag.

5 Place coated chicken on a plate and repeat with remaining chicken strips.

6 Fill deep fryer with oil per manufacturer directions and heat to 350°F, or in a 5½-quart Dutch oven add enough oil to fill pot by 3 inches, leaving at least 3 inches of space at the top, and place over medium-high heat until oil reaches 350°F.

7 Fry chicken strips in oil in batches so they do not touch, turning, about 4–5 minutes until strips are golden brown and they float and reach an internal temperature of 165°F.

8 Drain on paper towels. Serve hot.

California Pizza Kitchen
The Original BBQ Chicken Pizza

SERVES 4

This signature CPK pizza has been on the menu since the restaurant was founded in 1985. If you want to dress up your pizza, add 1/3 cup chopped cooked bacon or 1/3 cup chopped pineapple before baking.

8 ounces prepared refrigerated pizza dough

1 cup chopped grilled chicken breast strips

¾ cup barbecue sauce, divided

½ cup shredded mozzarella cheese

½ cup shredded smoked Gouda cheese

⅓ cup thin-sliced red onion

3 tablespoons chopped fresh cilantro

1 Remove dough from refrigerator and place on a 12-inch pizza pan sprayed with nonstick cooking spray. Cover with a damp towel and let rest at room temperature 30 minutes.

2 While dough rests, preheat oven to 450°F.

3 In a medium bowl, combine chicken with ¼ cup barbecue sauce. Toss to evenly coat. Set aside.

4 Once rested, stretch pizza dough into a 12-inch circle in pan. Spread remaining barbecue sauce over crust, leaving a ½-inch rim around crust. Sprinkle crust with mozzarella cheese, smoked Gouda, chicken, red onion, and cilantro.

5 Bake pizza 10–12 minutes until cheese is bubbling and crust is golden brown on sides and bottom. Remove from oven and let stand 5 minutes before slicing and serving.

CALIFORNIA PIZZA KITCHEN THE ORIGINAL BBQ CHICKEN PIZZA

Carrabba's Italian Grill Meatballs

This simple restaurant copycat recipe for meatballs tastes just like the ones served at Carrabba's. It uses a combination of meats and tastes so good it will make you happy that you decided to stay in and cook.

SERVES 6

1 pound ground beef

½ pound ground pork

⅓ cup plain bread crumbs

4 cloves garlic, minced

2 large eggs

2 medium green onions, minced

1 small yellow onion, peeled and minced

3 tablespoons grated Parmesan cheese

3 tablespoons grated Romano cheese

3 tablespoons minced fresh parsley

3 tablespoons minced fresh basil

½ teaspoon salt

½ teaspoon ground black pepper

½ cup olive oil, divided

1 Preheat oven to 400°F.

2 Combine all ingredients except olive oil in a large bowl. Mix with a wooden spoon or hands until just combined. Do not overmix.

3 Roll mixture into 1½-inch balls.

4 Pour ¼ cup olive oil into a 13-inch × 9-inch baking pan and place meatballs in pan. Drizzle remaining oil over meatballs.

5 Bake 25–30 minutes until meatballs are golden brown and reach an internal temperature of at least 165°F.

6 Remove meatballs from pan and drain on a paper towel–lined plate. Enjoy hot.

The Cheesecake Factory Bang-Bang Chicken and Shrimp

SERVES 2

This Thai-inspired dish is one of the post popular at The Cheesecake Factory, it is easy to make it at home!

Sauce

¼ cup creamy peanut butter

1 tablespoon vegetable oil

2 teaspoons soy sauce

2 teaspoons lime juice

1 teaspoon granulated sugar

1 teaspoon rice vinegar

Curry

1 tablespoon vegetable oil

2 tablespoons Thai red curry paste, such as A Taste of Thai

1 large carrot, peeled and julienned

1 medium zucchini, julienned

1 (14-ounce) can full-fat coconut milk

1 (6-ounce) boneless, skinless chicken breast, cut into ⅛-inch strips

12 large shrimp, peeled and deveined

½ cup frozen peas

Assembly

1 cup cooked white rice

¼ cup chopped unsalted peanuts

2 tablespoons toasted shredded coconut

2 teaspoons toasted sesame seeds

1 medium green onion, green part only, thinly sliced

1 For the sauce: In a 1-quart saucepan, combine all ingredients. Whisk until combined and smooth. Heat over low heat until warmed through and sugar has dissolved. Set aside.

2 For the curry: In a 10-inch skillet over medium heat, add oil. Once hot, add curry paste and cook 30 seconds, then add carrot and zucchini and sauté 1 minute to soften. Stir in coconut milk.

3 Bring mixture to a simmer, add chicken, and cook 5 minutes, then add shrimp and peas and cook 5 minutes more or until shrimp are cooked through and curled into a "C" shape.

4 For the assembly: Place rice in a mound in center of each serving plate. Divide curry between plates, then drizzle with sauce. Garnish with peanuts, coconut, sesame seeds, and green onion. Serve hot.

Chili's Margarita Grilled Chicken

The popular and unique Margarita Grilled Chicken on the menu at Chili's is quite easy to make at home and pairs perfectly with Chili's Presidente Margarita from Chapter 11.

1 cup liquid margarita mix

4 (6-ounce) boneless, skinless chicken breasts

½ teaspoon ground black pepper

2 tablespoons vegetable oil

2 cups canned black beans, heated per package instructions

1 cup tortilla strips

1 cup prepared pico de gallo

1 Pour margarita mix into a large resealable plastic bag. Add chicken breasts and marinate 2 hours in refrigerator.

2 Remove chicken from marinade, pat dry, and season with pepper.

3 Heat a 10-inch skillet to medium-high heat. Once hot, add oil and swirl to coat pan.

4 Cook chicken 3–4 minutes per side until it reaches an internal temperature of 165°F. Remove from pan and rest 3 minutes, then cut each breast into four pieces each.

5 Add ½ cup beans to each of four serving plates, then top with four chicken strips, ¼ cup tortilla strips, and ¼ cup pico de gallo. Serve immediately.

SERVES 4

CHILI'S

Chili's is a large casual dining chain founded in Dallas, Texas, that boasts more than 1,200 restaurants in the US. They serve American food with a Southwest influence. The menu offers salads, fajitas, and quesadillas as well as traditional American steaks, ribs, and hamburgers.

Chipotle Beef Barbacoa

SERVES 12

Chipotle is known for its large burritos using all-natural ingredients with a choice of chicken, pork, steak, or beef chuck roast. Their barbacoa is beef that is braised in spices until tender and juicy.

2 medium yellow onions, peeled and diced

3 tablespoons olive oil

8 cloves garlic, minced

1 tablespoon taco seasoning

1½ tablespoons dried oregano

1 (0.36-ounce) can chipotle in adobo sauce

1 cup beef broth

1 cup water

1 dried bay leaf

2 tablespoons white vinegar

3 pounds beef chuck roast

1 Place all ingredients except chuck roast in a blender. Blend 1–2 minutes until smooth.

2 Add a third of the blended sauce to bottom of a slow cooker.

3 Place chuck roast in slow cooker pot and pour remaining sauce over meat.

4 Cook 8–10 hours on low. Once cooked, remove bay leaf then gently shred meat in cooking liquid. Serve hot.

Chipotle Carnitas

Mexican pork carnitas are slow-cooked, spicy strips of pork shoulder meat traditionally served with tortillas and salsa. Make this a day ahead to let the flavors really develop.

SERVES 10

1 (3-pound) pork shoulder roast

½ teaspoon salt

½ teaspoon ground black pepper

3 tablespoons vegetable oil

1 large yellow onion, peeled and thinly sliced

4 medium Roma tomatoes

½ teaspoon dried oregano

1 teaspoon ground cumin

2 dried bay leaves

2 whole cloves

2 dried chipotle chilies

¾ cup water

1 Preheat oven to 325°F.

2 Season pork with salt and pepper. Allow to come to room temperature, about 40 minutes.

3 Heat a large ovenproof Dutch oven over medium-high heat. Once hot, add oil. Sear pork 5 minutes per side. Remove pork from pan and let rest 10–15 minutes.

4 To same pan over medium heat, add onion and cook 2–3 minutes until translucent. Return pork to pan and add remaining ingredients.

5 Cover pan with a lid and place in oven. Cook 3 hours or until pork reaches an internal temperature of 180°F–190°F.

6 Let pork rest in cooking liquid 10–15 minutes.

7 Preheat oven to 450°F. Place pork on an ungreased half baking sheet and spoon cooking liquid over pork so all pork is coated. Bake 20 minutes, shredding and stirring pork every 5 minutes as it cooks and becomes crusty. Add additional cooking liquid if pork becomes dry. Remove from oven, remove bay leaves, and cool 5 minutes. Serve hot.

Chipotle Chicken

Once cooked, you can keep this chicken in the refrigerator for up to 5 days to have burritos and bowls any time.

1 (2-ounce) package dried ancho chilies

6 cloves garlic

½ large red onion, peeled and quartered

¼ cup vegetable oil

2 tablespoons chopped fresh oregano

2 teaspoons ground cumin

1 teaspoon ground black pepper

4 (6-ounce) boneless, skinless chicken breasts

1　Soak dried chilies overnight in water until soft. Remove seeds.
2　Place chilies, garlic, red onion, oil, oregano, cumin, and pepper in a food processor and purée until smooth.
3　In a medium baking dish, add chicken and spread chili marinade over top. Turn chicken to coat evenly.
4　Refrigerate at least 1 hour or up to 24 hours.
5　Preheat outdoor barbecue or smokeless indoor grill to medium-high heat.
6　Remove chicken from marinade and place on grill. Cook 5 minutes per side or until chicken reaches an internal temperature of 165°F. Remove from grill, cover with foil, and rest for 5 minutes before serving.

Cracker Barrel Grilled Chicken Tenders

Serve these savory, juicy tenders with Cracker Barrel Green Beans and Cracker Barrel Carrots (see Chapter 9) for a full meal.

½ cup Italian dressing

1 teaspoon fresh lime juice

1½ teaspoons honey

1 pound chicken breast tenders

1　In a medium bowl, mix together dressing, lime juice, and honey. Pour mixture over chicken tenders, making sure all chicken is covered. Marinate 1 hour in refrigerator.
2　Preheat indoor smokeless grill to 350°F or heat a grill pan to medium.
3　Grill chicken to a light golden color and an internal temperature of 165°F, about 2–3 minutes per side. Remove from grill and let rest 3 minutes before serving.

Jack in the Box Tacos

These tacos have been on the menu since the 1950s, and while they are not gourmet, they are delicious after an evening out or when you need the comfort only spicy, greasy food can provide.

SERVES 4

8 ounces 80/20 ground beef

½ teaspoon taco seasoning

1 cup canned refried beans

8 (6-inch) yellow corn tortillas

4 slices American cheese

½ cup vegetable oil, divided

2 cups shredded iceberg lettuce

½ cup mild taco sauce

1 In a 10-inch skillet over medium heat, add ground beef. Cook, crumbling well, until browned, about 5 minutes. Add taco seasoning and stir well to mix. Remove from heat and add beans. Stir well to combine. Set aside.

2 Wrap tortillas in a damp towel. Microwave on high 30 seconds, then flip and microwave on high 15 seconds more or until tortillas are soft and flexible.

3 Spread bean and meat mixture evenly between tortillas. Add ½ slice cheese to each tortilla and fold tortilla in half.

4 To same skillet over medium heat, add ¼ cup oil. Once hot, add tacos four at a time and cook 2–3 minutes per side, or until tacos are crisp around edges. Remove tacos to a paper towel–lined plate to drain and repeat with remaining oil and tacos.

5 Once tacos have cooled 2 minutes, gently open and divide lettuce and taco sauce between them. Serve hot.

LongHorn Steakhouse Outlaw Ribeye

SERVES 2

LONGHORN STEAKHOUSE

LongHorn Steakhouse is a restaurant chain with more than 500 locations and a western/Texas theme. They are best known for serving various kinds of grilled steaks, but they also grill fresh fish and chicken.

This large bone-in steak is juicy, tender, and more than enough to feed two people or one very hungry person. This makes an impressive date-night-at-home dinner or a part of a special celebration dinner.

1 teaspoon salt

½ teaspoon ground black pepper

⅛ teaspoon onion powder

⅛ teaspoon garlic powder

⅛ teaspoon ground cumin

⅛ teaspoon dried thyme

⅛ teaspoon paprika

1 (20-ounce) bone-in USDA choice rib eye

1 In a small bowl, combine salt, pepper, onion powder, garlic powder, cumin, thyme, and paprika. Mix well to combine. If thyme leaves are very large, rub them between your fingers to break into smaller pieces.

2 Remove steak from refrigerator 30 minutes before grilling to allow it to come to room temperature.

3 Preheat outdoor barbecue or indoor smokeless grill to medium-high heat.

4 Season steak on both sides with prepared seasoning. Grill 4–5 minutes per side for medium-rare (until steak reaches an internal temperature of 130°F), 6–7 minutes per side for medium (135°F), 8–9 minutes per side for medium-well (145°F), or 10 minutes per side for well-done (155°F).

5 Remove steak from grill and let rest 3 minutes before serving. Enjoy hot.

LONGHORN STEAKHOUSE OUTLAW RIBEYE

LongHorn Steakhouse Parmesan Crusted Chicken

Parmesan Crusted Chicken is one of the specialty items on the LongHorn Steakhouse menu. It is a popular choice for those wanting to indulge in a steakhouse meal but without the steak.

Chicken

2 (8-ounce) boneless, skinless chicken breasts

¼ cup ranch dressing

2 tablespoons olive oil

2 teaspoons lemon juice

2 teaspoons Worcestershire sauce

1 clove garlic, minced

½ teaspoon ground black pepper

Parmesan Crust

⅓ cup ranch dressing

½ cup grated Parmesan cheese, divided

⅓ cup grated provolone cheese

4 tablespoons salted butter, melted

¾ cup panko bread crumbs

½ teaspoon garlic powder

1 For the chicken: Place chicken breasts between two pieces of wax paper. Pound with a meat mallet until chicken is ½-inch thick.

2 Add remaining ingredients to a large resealable plastic bag. Massage bag to combine, then add chicken and massage to evenly coat. Seal bag and marinate 2 hours in refrigerator.

3 Preheat outdoor barbecue or indoor smokeless grill to medium-high heat. Preheat broiler to 500°F.

4 Remove chicken from marinade and transfer to grill. Cook 4–5 minutes per side until chicken reaches an internal temperature of 165°F. Transfer chicken breasts to an ungreased quarter baking sheet.

5 For the Parmesan crust: While chicken grills, combine ranch dressing, ⅓ cup Parmesan cheese, and provolone in a small bowl and mix well.

6 In a separate small bowl, combine remaining Parmesan cheese, butter, panko, and garlic powder. Mix until panko is evenly coated.

7 Spread cheese mixture over chicken breasts. Sprinkle with panko. Broil 3–4 minutes until panko is toasted and golden brown. Serve immediately.

Panda Express Beijing Beef

In March 2008, Panda Express added Beijing Beef to their menu. It was a notable event as it was their first major new menu item since 1987. It is one of the restaurant chain's most popular menu items.

SERVES 4

1 large egg

¼ teaspoon salt

3 ounces water, divided

7 tablespoons plus 2 teaspoons cornstarch, divided

1 tablespoon all-purpose flour

1 pound flank steak, sliced into thin strips

4 tablespoons granulated sugar

3 tablespoons ketchup

2 tablespoons vinegar

¼ teaspoon crushed chili pepper

Vegetable oil, for frying, plus 2 tablespoons, divided

1 medium red bell pepper, seeded and diced

1 medium green bell pepper, seeded and diced

1 medium white onion, peeled and sliced

1 teaspoon minced garlic

SLICING BEEF

Most Chinese recipes call for thin cuts, or strips, of meat. It is much easier to make thin cuts if the meat is partially frozen by putting it in the freezer for 20–30 minutes. Cut meat across the grain; it will be easier to eat and have a better appearance.

1 In a large bowl or resealable plastic bag, combine egg, salt, 2 tablespoons water, 1 tablespoon cornstarch, and flour and mix well. Add beef slices and allow to marinate 15 minutes.

2 In a small bowl, mix together remaining water, sugar, ketchup, vinegar, chili pepper, and 2 teaspoons cornstarch and refrigerate until ready to use. Place remaining cornstarch in a small, shallow dish.

3 Fill deep fryer with oil per manufacturer directions and heat to 350°F, or in a 5½-quart Dutch oven add enough oil to fill pot by 3 inches, leaving at least 3 inches of space at the top, and place over medium-high heat until oil reaches 350°F.

4 When beef is done marinating, coat slices in cornstarch. Remove any excess cornstarch and then deep-fry beef in batches until beef is floating or golden brown, about 2–3 minutes. Transfer to a paper towel–lined plate to drain.

5 Add 2 tablespoons oil to wok over high heat. Once hot, add peppers and onion and stir-fry 2 minutes. Add garlic and stir-fry 30 seconds. Remove vegetables and set aside.

6 Pour prepared sauce into wok and heat, stirring constantly, until boiling and thickened. Add vegetables and beef and toss quickly to coat in sauce. Transfer to a serving platter and serve immediately.

Panda Express Orange Chicken

SERVES 6

PANDA EXPRESS

Panda Express, with over 2,000 restaurants, is the largest chain of Chinese fast-food restaurants in the US. No MSG is added to any item on the menu. They offer a "create your own combo" meal whereby you choose a two- or three-entrée plate, and they offer quite a few low-calorie options.

Panda Express has lots of great dishes, but none is as legendary as their Orange Chicken. This restaurant copycat recipe lets you make your own version of their delicious favorite.

Vegetable oil, for frying, plus 1 tablespoon, divided

1 large egg

⅛ teaspoon salt

⅛ teaspoon ground black pepper

½ cup plus 1 tablespoon cornstarch, divided

¼ cup all-purpose flour

2 pounds boneless, skinless chicken breasts, cut into 1-inch pieces

1 teaspoon sesame oil

1 teaspoon minced ginger

1 teaspoon minced garlic

¼ teaspoon red pepper flakes

¼ cup chopped green onions

Zest from 1 medium orange

1½ tablespoons soy sauce

5 tablespoons granulated sugar

5 tablespoons white vinegar

1 tablespoon rice wine

2 tablespoons water

1 Fill deep fryer with oil per manufacturer directions and heat to 375°F, or in a 5½-quart Dutch oven add enough oil to fill pot by 3 inches, leaving at least 3 inches of space at the top, and place over medium-high heat until oil reaches 375°F.

2 In a medium bowl, add egg, salt, black pepper, and 1 tablespoon oil, and mix well. Add ½ cup cornstarch and flour and mix well. Add chicken to mixture and coat well.

3 Transfer chicken pieces five or six at a time to hot oil. Fry 3–4 minutes until chicken is golden brown and reaches an internal temperature of 165°F. Transfer to a paper towel–lined plate to drain. Repeat with remaining chicken. Set aside.

4 In a 10-inch skillet over medium heat, add sesame oil, ginger, and garlic. Heat 10–20 seconds until fragrant. Add red pepper flakes and green onions and sauté 15 seconds. Add orange zest, soy sauce, sugar, vinegar, and rice wine and bring to a boil.

5 In a small bowl, add water to remaining cornstarch and mix well. Combine cornstarch mixture with sauce mixture in pan and heat until sauce has thickened, about 5 minutes. Add chicken and toss to coat in sauce. Remove from heat and serve immediately.

P.F. Chang's BBQ Pork Spare Ribs

One of the most popular dishes on P.F. Chang's appetizer menu is the spareribs that come slathered with an Asian barbecue sauce.

SERVES 2

1 cup ketchup

1 cup light corn syrup

½ cup hoisin sauce

½ cup water

⅓ cup packed light brown sugar

2 tablespoons minced onions

1 tablespoon rice vinegar

12–16 cups water

2 teaspoons salt

1 rack pork spareribs

4 cups vegetable oil

1 teaspoon sesame seeds

1 tablespoon diced green onion

1 In a medium saucepan over medium heat, combine ketchup, corn syrup, hoisin sauce, water, brown sugar, onions, and vinegar. Bring mixture to a boil, then reduce heat to medium-low and simmer 5 minutes or until thick. Cool.

2 Heat water in a large saucepan or Dutch oven over high heat. Add salt.

3 As water comes to a boil, trim excess fat and slice between bones of each rib to separate. Toss ribs in boiling water and boil 12–14 minutes. Remove ribs to a plate to cool.

4 In a separate large saucepan over medium heat, heat oil to 375°F.

5 Add four to six ribs at a time to hot oil and fry 2–4 minutes until browned. Drain on a rack or paper towel–lined plate. Repeat with remaining ribs.

6 Once ribs are browned, heat a wok over medium heat. When hot, add ribs and prepared sauce, tossing ribs to coat. Simmer ribs in sauce, stirring often, about 1 minute. Remove to a serving plate. Sprinkle ribs with sesame seeds and green onion. Serve hot.

P.F. Chang's Chicken Lettuce Wraps

SERVES 6

Lettuce wraps are the most popular menu item at P.F. Chang's. They are a delightful mix of crisp, cool lettuce and a savory hot filling made of quickly cooked spiced chicken and vegetables.

8 dried shiitake mushrooms

1 tablespoon hoisin sauce

1 tablespoon plus 2 teaspoons soy sauce, divided

1 tablespoon plus 2 teaspoons dry sherry, divided

2 tablespoons oyster sauce

2 tablespoons plus 2 teaspoons water, divided

1 teaspoon sesame oil, divided

1 teaspoon granulated sugar

2 teaspoons plus 1 teaspoon cornstarch, divided

1/4 teaspoon salt

1/4 teaspoon ground black pepper

1 1/2 pounds boneless, skinless chicken breasts

5 tablespoons vegetable oil, divided

1 teaspoon minced fresh ginger

2 cloves garlic, minced

2 small dried chilies

2 medium green onions, minced

1 (8-ounce) can bamboo shoots, drained and minced

1 (8-ounce) can water chestnuts, drained and minced

1 (1-pound) package prepared Chinese rice noodles

6 large iceberg lettuce leaves

1 Cover mushrooms with boiling water, let stand 30 minutes, then drain. Cut and discard stems and then mince mushrooms. Set aside.

2 In a medium bowl, mix together hoisin sauce, 1 tablespoon soy sauce, 1 tablespoon sherry, oyster sauce, 1 tablespoon water, sesame oil, sugar, and 2 teaspoons cornstarch. Set aside.

3 In another medium bowl, combine remaining cornstarch, remaining sherry, remaining soy sauce, remaining water, salt, pepper, and chicken. Stir to coat chicken thoroughly. Stir in 1 teaspoon vegetable oil and marinate chicken 15 minutes.

4 Heat a wok or 10-inch skillet over medium-high heat. Add 3 tablespoons vegetable oil, then add chicken and stir-fry 3–4 minutes. Transfer chicken to a plate and set aside.

5 Add remaining vegetable oil to pan. Add ginger, garlic, chilies, and green onions and stir-fry, about 1 minute.

6 Add mushrooms, bamboo shoots, and water chestnuts and stir-fry an additional 2 minutes.

7 Return chicken to pan. Add prepared sauce and cook 5 minutes or until thickened and hot.

8 Break noodles into small pieces and add to a serving dish to cover bottom. Pour chicken mixture over top. Divide chicken mixture and noodles evenly between lettuce leaves and roll, then serve.

P.F. Chang's Mongolian Beef

SERVES 4

One of the reasons P.F. Chang's tastes so good is that each restaurant makes their food from scratch. This version is also made from scratch so you can enjoy the same flavor at home.

1 cup plus 2 teaspoons vegetable oil, divided

½ teaspoon minced ginger

1 tablespoon chopped garlic

½ cup soy sauce

½ cup water

¾ cup packed dark brown sugar

1 pound flank steak

¼ cup cornstarch

2 large green onions

1. In a 2-quart saucepan over medium heat, add 2 teaspoons oil. Once hot, add ginger and garlic and cook 10 seconds, then add soy sauce and water.

2. Add brown sugar and stir until dissolved. Raise heat to high and boil 2–3 minutes until sauce thickens. Remove from heat.

3. Slice steak against grain into ¼-inch-thick bite-sized pieces. Dip pieces in cornstarch and toss to coat all sides. Let sit 10 minutes so cornstarch adheres.

4. As beef sits, heat remaining oil in a wok over medium heat until it reaches 350°F.

5. Add beef to oil and fry, stirring occasionally, 2 minutes or until beef just begins to darken at edges. Transfer beef to a paper towel–lined plate to drain. Pour oil out of wok.

6. Place wok back over medium heat and add prepared sauce. Cook, stirring constantly, 1 minute. Add beef and toss to coat evenly. Add green onions and cook 1 minute. Remove beef and green onions with tongs or a slotted spoon to a serving plate. Serve hot.

Pizza Hut Original Stuffed Crust Pizza

Created in 1995, stuffed crust pizza took America by storm! Here is a quick and easy way to re-create stuffed crust pizza like Pizza Hut's using ready-made refrigerated pizza dough from your deli counter and string cheese.

SERVES 6

16 ounces prepared refrigerated pizza dough

7 pieces string cheese

2 teaspoons olive oil

½ cup marinara sauce

2 cups shredded mozzarella cheese

24 slices pepperoni

1 Remove dough from refrigerator and transfer to a medium bowl. Cover with plastic wrap and let stand at room temperature 1 hour.

2 Preheat oven to 425°F.

3 Roll out dough on a floured surface into an 18-inch circle. Place on a pizza pan.

4 Place a ring of string cheese end to end all the way around edge of dough.

5 Fold edge of dough up and over cheese and press firmly, forming a crust ring. Brush top of folded dough with olive oil.

6 Cover center of pizza with sauce, cheese, and pepperoni. Bake 12–16 minutes until crust browns and cheese has melted. Let cool 5 minutes before slicing.

Popeyes Signature Chicken

SERVES 8

Founded in 1972 in New Orleans, Popeyes is a famous quick-service restaurant chain popular for its spicy Louisiana-style fried chicken, biscuits, and Cajun-inspired sides.

3 cups all-purpose flour

1 cup cornstarch

3 tablespoons seasoned salt

3 tablespoons granulated sugar

2 tablespoons paprika

2 tablespoons Cajun seasoning

1 teaspoon baking soda

3 cups crushed cornflakes

2 large eggs

¼ cup cold water

Vegetable oil, for frying

4 pounds bone-in chicken pieces

1 In a large bowl, combine flour, cornstarch, seasoned salt, sugar, paprika, Cajun seasoning, and baking soda. Whisk to combine.

2 In a second large bowl, add cornflakes.

3 In a third large bowl, beat eggs and water.

4 Fill deep fryer with oil per manufacturer directions and heat to 350°F, or in a 5½-quart Dutch oven add enough oil to fill pot by 3 inches, leaving at least 3 inches of space at the top, and place over medium-high heat until oil reaches 350°F.

5 Grease a 9-inch × 12-inch × 2-inch baking pan and set aside. Preheat oven to 350°F.

6 Dip chicken pieces 1 at a time first in dry coating mix, then in egg and water mix, then in cornflakes, and briefly back in dry mix.

7 Drop chicken pieces in hot oil, skin side down, and brown 3–4 minutes over medium-high heat. Turn and brown other side. Don't crowd pieces during frying.

8 Place chicken pieces in prepared pan in a single layer, skin side up. Cover pan with foil, leaving one side loose for steam to escape.

9 Bake 35–40 minutes, then remove foil and bake uncovered 5 minutes more to crisp coating. Serve immediately.

Taco Bell Crunchwrap Supreme

One of Taco Bell's most popular items, the Crunchwrap Supreme traditionally comes with ground beef, but you can also make a vegetarian version by swapping the beef for canned seasoned black beans.

SERVES 4

½ pound 80/20 ground beef

½ teaspoon salt

¼ teaspoon dried minced onion

½ (1-ounce) packet taco seasoning

2 tablespoons water

5 (12-inch) flour tortillas

1 cup nacho cheese sauce

4 corn tostada shells

2 cups shredded iceberg lettuce

1 cup diced tomatoes

1 cup full-fat sour cream

1 In a 10-inch skillet over medium heat, add ground beef. Cook 7–10 minutes until browned. Drain fat from pan, then add salt, onion, taco seasoning, and water. Let mixture simmer over medium heat 10 minutes, stirring often.

2 Heat a griddle over medium heat.

3 Warm tortillas in microwave 20–30 seconds until tortillas are warm and flexible.

4 Cut 1 tortilla into four wedges. Place remaining tortillas on a work surface. Divide ground beef and cheese sauce evenly among tortillas, placing in center of each tortilla. Top each with a tostada shell, lettuce, tomatoes, and sour cream. Center a wedge of tortilla on top, then fold bottom tortilla edges up and over center as tightly as possible.

5 Place wraps seam side down on heated griddle. Work in batches if all wraps do not fit on griddle. Cook 2–3 minutes until golden brown, then flip and cook second side 2 minutes. Transfer to serving plates and enjoy immediately.

TACO BELL CRUNCHWRAP SUPREME

Taco Bell Mexican Pizza

This fan favorite was created in 1985 but despite its popularity was removed from Taco Bell's menu in 2020. Fans started a petition and their demand ultimately saw its return in 2022!

SERVES 4

½ pound 80/20 ground beef

½ teaspoon salt

¼ teaspoon dried minced onion

½ (1-ounce) packet taco seasoning

2 tablespoons water

1 cup vegetable oil

8 (6-inch) flour tortillas

1 (16-ounce) can refried beans

½ cup mild salsa

2 cups shredded Cheddar cheese

2 cups shredded Monterey jack cheese

⅓ cup diced tomato

1 Preheat oven to 400°F.

2 In a 10-inch skillet over medium heat, add ground beef. Cook 7–10 minutes until browned. Drain fat from pan, then add salt, onion, taco seasoning, and water. Let mixture simmer over medium heat 10 minutes, stirring often.

3 Heat oil in another 10-inch skillet over medium-high heat to 350°F.

4 Fry each tortilla in hot oil about 30–45 seconds per side until golden brown. Transfer to a paper towel–lined plate to drain.

5 Add refried beans to a medium microwave-safe bowl and microwave 1–2 minutes until steaming hot.

6 Place 4 tortillas on an ungreased half baking sheet. Spread ⅓ cup beans on each tortilla. Next add ⅓ cup meat and ¼ cup each Cheddar and Monterey jack cheese, then top with 1 tortilla each.

7 Top tortillas with 2 tablespoons salsa each, then divide remaining cheeses evenly over top of salsa. Bake 8–12 minutes until cheeses are melted. Garnish with tomato. Enjoy hot.

TGI Fridays Sizzling Chicken & Cheese

SERVES 2

Well-known around the world for American-style bar food, TGI Fridays boasts more than 600 locations around the world. This recipe is served sizzling in a hot skillet, so be careful when enjoying.

2 (4-ounce) boneless, skinless chicken breasts

2 tablespoons chopped garlic

2 tablespoons chopped fresh parsley

1 teaspoon crushed red pepper flakes

¼ teaspoon ground black pepper

¼ teaspoon salt

4 tablespoons olive oil, divided

1 medium green bell pepper, seeded and julienned

1 medium red bell pepper, seeded and julienned

1 medium yellow onion, peeled and julienned

4 cups cooked mashed potatoes

½ cup shredded Chihuahua white cheese

2 slices American cheese

1 Pound chicken breasts between two pieces of wax paper with a meat mallet to ½-inch thickness.

2 In a large resealable plastic bag, combine garlic, parsley, red pepper flakes, black pepper, salt, and 2 tablespoons olive oil. Place chicken breasts in marinade and refrigerate 2–4 hours.

3 In a 10-inch cast iron skillet over medium heat, heat remaining olive oil. Add chicken breasts and cook 5 minutes per side until chicken reaches an internal temperature of 165°F and is golden brown. Remove from pan.

4 To same skillet over medium heat, add bell peppers and onion and cook 2–3 minutes until just tender. Remove from skillet.

5 Heat a separate 10-inch cast iron skillet over high heat. Place mashed potatoes in half of skillet, then add cheeses, bell peppers, and onion to other half.

6 Place chicken on top of potatoes. Serve hot directly in skillet.

Wendy's Chili con Carne

Wendy's prides themselves on serving fresh-cooked burgers. What happens to burgers that linger too long on the flattop grill? They are used to make Wendy's famous chili!

SERVES 4

1 pound 80/20 ground beef

½ teaspoon salt

½ teaspoon ground black pepper

1 tablespoon vegetable oil

1 medium yellow onion, peeled and chopped

1 medium green bell pepper, seeded and chopped

1 medium stalk celery, chopped

1 (1.25-ounce) packet chili seasoning

2 teaspoons granulated sugar

1 teaspoon onion powder

1 teaspoon garlic powder

½ teaspoon smoked paprika

1 (8-ounce) can tomato sauce

1 (14.5-ounce) can diced tomatoes, undrained

1 cup beef broth

1 (14.5-ounce) can kidney beans, drained and rinsed

1 Preheat outdoor barbecue or indoor smokeless grill to medium-high heat.

2 Form ground beef into six patties and season both sides with salt and black pepper. Place patties on heated grill and cook until they reach an internal temperature of 165°F, about 5 minutes per side. Allow to cool, then chop into ½-inch pieces. Set aside.

3 In a 3-quart saucepan over medium heat, add oil. Once hot, add onion, bell pepper, and celery. Sauté 5 minutes or until tender. Add chili seasoning and cook 30 seconds or until fragrant, then add sugar, onion powder, garlic powder, and paprika and stir well.

4 Stir in tomato sauce and diced tomatoes and scrape bottom of pan to release any brown bits. Stir in beef broth, then bring mixture to a boil. Once boiling, reduce heat to low and stir in beef and beans. Cover pan with a lid and simmer 20 minutes, then remove lid and simmer 30–40 minutes more until chili is thickened to your preference. Remove from heat and serve hot.

CHAPTER 7

Seafood and Vegetarian Entrées

Golden Corral Seafood Salad

SERVES 6

This dish is perfect for a light lunch or dinner and may be served on top of salad greens, in a tortilla wrap, or on bread as a seafood sandwich.

1 pound shredded imitation crabmeat

1 cup diced celery

½ cup mayonnaise

¼ cup diced green onions

1 tablespoon lemon juice

3 large hardboiled eggs, peeled and chopped

1. Mix all ingredients together in a medium-sized bowl with a lid.
2. Cover bowl and refrigerate at least 1 hour before serving to allow flavors to blend.

Long John Silver's Fish

SERVES 2

The secret to the Long John Silver's taste is the beer batter they dip their fish, chicken, and shrimp into before frying. The best type of fish to use is pollock, cod, or firm whitefish.

Vegetable oil, for frying

1 cup McCormick Golden Dipt Beer Batter Seafood Batter Mix

⅔ cup beer

1½ pounds pollock fillets, cut into serving-sized pieces

1. Fill deep fryer with oil per manufacturer directions and heat to 350°F, or in a 5½-quart Dutch oven add enough oil to fill pot by 3 inches, leaving at least 3 inches of space at the top, and place over medium-high heat until oil reaches 350°F.
2. In a medium bowl, stir batter mix and beer until smooth.
3. Dip fish in batter and shake off any excess.
4. Carefully add fish a few pieces at a time to hot oil. Fry 3–5 minutes, turning once to brown evenly. Fish is done when it is golden brown and flakes easily with a fork. Drain fried fish on paper towels. Serve.

Long John Silver's Fish Tacos

Long John Silver's added Fish Tacos to their menu in 2009. The sauce adds a zesty flavor that gives this taco its kick. You can substitute grilled fish for a light alternative.

SERVES 1

Sauce

½ cup full-fat sour cream

½ cup mayonnaise

2 teaspoons taco seasoning

1 small jalapeño, diced

¼ cup fresh lime juice

½ cup chopped fresh cilantro

Taco

2 (6-inch) flour tortillas

2 fillets Long John Silver's Fish (see recipe in this chapter)

½ cup shredded lettuce

1 For the sauce: Combine all ingredients in a small bowl. Mix well and set aside.

2 For the taco: Heat flour tortillas in microwave 20 seconds to soften.

3 Place 1 fish fillet in center of each tortilla. Add lettuce to each and drizzle with sauce. Fold in half and serve immediately.

LONG JOHN SILVER'S FISH TACOS

Outback Steakhouse Gold Coast Coconut Shrimp

Coconut-crusted deep-fried shrimp is a popular appetizer ahead of a steakhouse dinner, but you can also enjoy these for a main meal served along with a green salad or with KFC Cole Slaw (see Chapter 9).

SERVES 2

Dipping Sauce

½ cup orange marmalade

2 tablespoons Thai sweet chili sauce

1 teaspoon Cajun seasoning

½ teaspoon white horseradish sauce

⅛ teaspoon Tabasco sauce

Shrimp

1 (7-ounce) bag shredded coconut, divided

2 tablespoons granulated sugar

½ teaspoon salt

1 cup all-purpose flour

1 cup beer

Vegetable oil, for frying

12 tail-on jumbo shrimp, peeled and deveined

1 For the dipping sauce: Combine all ingredients in a small bowl. Chill in refrigerator at least 30 minutes before serving.

2 For the shrimp: In a medium bowl, combine ½ cup coconut, sugar, salt, flour, and beer. Mix well, cover, and refrigerate at least 1 hour.

3 Fill deep fryer with oil per manufacturer directions and heat to 350°F, or in a 5½-quart Dutch oven add enough oil to fill pot by 3 inches, leaving at least 3 inches of space at the top, and place over medium-high heat until oil reaches 350°F.

4 Pour remaining coconut into a shallow bowl. Dip 1 shrimp at a time in batter, then roll battered shrimp in coconut.

5 Fry shrimp a few at a time in hot oil 2–3 minutes until shrimp turn golden brown. Drain on a paper towel–lined plate. Repeat with remaining shrimp and batter. Serve immediately with dipping sauce.

Outback Steakhouse Grilled Shrimp on the Barbie

The name of this scrumptious grilled shrimp dish is synonymous with Australia, as the Australian Tourism Commission popularized the phrase "shrimp on the barbie" in a series of advertisements that aired in the US and UK in the 1980s.

Dipping Sauce

2 cups mayonnaise

2 cups sour cream

½ cup tomato chili sauce

½ teaspoon cayenne pepper

Shrimp

½ cup salted butter, melted

½ cup olive oil

½ cup minced fresh parsley

3 tablespoons fresh lemon juice

3 cloves garlic, crushed

1 tablespoon minced shallot

½ teaspoon salt

½ teaspoon ground black pepper

1½ pounds medium to large shrimp, unpeeled

1 For the dipping sauce: In a small bowl, combine all ingredients and mix well. Refrigerate until ready to serve.

2 For the shrimp: In a large bowl, combine butter, olive oil, parsley, lemon juice, garlic, shallot, salt, and black pepper. Mix in shrimp and allow to marinate in refrigerator 5 hours.

3 Preheat outdoor barbecue or indoor smokeless grill to 350°F.

4 Thread shrimp onto wood skewers. Grill shrimp, about 2 minutes per side. Serve shrimp hot with dipping sauce.

Panda Express Honey Walnut Shrimp

Added to the Panda Express menu in 2010, Honey Walnut Shrimp coats crispy fried shrimp in a sweet sauce and serves it with crisp candied walnuts. That same year, the dish won the MenuMasters award for Best New Menu Item!

Vegetable oil, for frying

4 large egg whites

¼ teaspoon salt

¼ cup cornstarch

1 pound large shrimp, peeled and deveined

¼ cup Japanese mayonnaise, such as Kewpie

12 tablespoons sweetened condensed milk

1 tablespoon honey

1 cup candied walnuts

1 Fill deep fryer with oil per manufacturer directions and heat to 350°F, or in a 5½-quart Dutch oven add enough oil to fill pot by 3 inches, leaving at least 3 inches of space at the top, and place over medium-high heat until oil reaches 350°F.

2 In a medium bowl, add egg whites and salt. Whisk until foamy, then add cornstarch and whisk until smooth.

3 Dip shrimp in cornstarch batter, letting excess drip off, then add to hot oil. Fry 4 or 5 shrimp at a time in oil 4 minutes or until crisp and golden brown. Transfer to a paper towel–lined plate and repeat with remaining shrimp and batter.

4 Add mayonnaise, condensed milk, and honey to a medium bowl and whisk to combine. Add shrimp and gently toss to coat.

5 Transfer shrimp to a serving plate and garnish with candied walnuts. Serve hot.

SERVES 4

CANDIED WALNUTS

To make candied walnuts: In a 12-inch nonstick skillet over medium heat, add 1 cup walnut halves, ¼ cup granulated sugar, and 1 tablespoon unsalted butter. Cook until sugar melts and coats walnuts thickly, about 5 minutes. Quickly transfer walnuts to parchment-lined half sheet pan and spread evenly. Cool completely before using.

PANDA EXPRESS HONEY WALNUT SHRIMP

P.F. Chang's Dynamite Shrimp

Do you love that firecracker shrimp you get in a Chinese restaurant? Then this delicious P.F. Chang's recipe will be one you'll want to try.

SERVES 2

2 tablespoons soy sauce

2 teaspoons granulated sugar

2 ounces water, divided

2 teaspoons white vinegar

1 teaspoon cornstarch

2 tablespoons canola oil

7 baby carrots, halved lengthwise

8 ounces large shrimp, peeled and deveined

½ cup sliced water chestnuts

24 snow peas

1 large clove garlic, chopped

1 large green onion, chopped

1 tablespoon chili paste

¼ teaspoon ground white pepper

2 teaspoons ground bean sauce

2 tablespoons sherry

2 tablespoons fresh chopped cilantro, for garnish

1 In a small bowl, combine soy sauce, sugar, 1 ounce water, and vinegar. Mix well and set aside.

2 In a separate small bowl, combine remaining water and cornstarch and set aside.

3 Heat a wok over high heat until smoking. Add oil and carrots and sauté 2 minutes or until color of carrots brightens.

4 Add shrimp and stir-fry 3 minutes or until about halfway cooked. Add water chestnuts, snow peas, and garlic. Sauté about 1 minute.

5 Add green onion, chili paste, pepper, and bean sauce. Cook until very fragrant, about 2 minutes, then reduce heat to low and add sherry. Cook for 20 seconds.

6 Increase heat to high and add soy sauce mixture and bring to a boil, about 2 minutes. Add cornstarch mixture and stir until thickened.

7 Garnish with cilantro. Serve immediately.

P.F. Chang's Stir-Fried Eggplant

SERVES 4

This vegetarian stir-fry recipe gives the eggplant a unique flavor with the addition of a fiery sauce and fresh green onion. If you can't get Chinese eggplant, you can use globe eggplant instead.

1 tablespoon cornstarch

4 tablespoons water, divided

2 tablespoons soy sauce

1 tablespoon white vinegar

1 tablespoon granulated sugar

1 teaspoon chili paste

½ teaspoon ground bean sauce

½ teaspoon sesame oil

1 tablespoon vegetable oil

1 pound Chinese eggplant, peeled and cut into 1-inch cubes

1 teaspoon minced garlic

¼ cup sliced green onion

1 In a small bowl, combine cornstarch and 2 tablespoons water to make a paste. Set aside.

2 In a separate small bowl, combine soy sauce, vinegar, sugar, chili paste, bean sauce, sesame oil, and remaining water. Mix well and set aside.

3 In a wok over high heat, add vegetable oil and fry eggplant cubes 1 minute. Remove and drain on paper towels.

4 Still over high heat, add garlic and stir-fry 5 seconds, then add prepared sauce. Reduce heat to low and let sauce simmer 20 seconds. Add eggplant cubes and simmer 10 seconds more.

5 Stir in cornstarch paste a little at a time until paste is the consistency of peanut butter. Stir in green onion. Serve immediately.

Red Lobster White Wine & Garlic Mussels

This dish is made with tender, fresh mussels cooked in a white wine sauce flavored with tomato, garlic, and lemon. You may want to serve this with extra slices of sourdough bread for soaking up the delicious cooling liquid!

SERVES 2

2 slices sourdough sandwich bread

3 tablespoons olive oil, divided

2 cloves garlic, minced

1 Roma tomato, seeded and diced

⅓ cup dry white wine

1 pound fresh mussels

2 tablespoons heavy cream

¼ teaspoon salt

¼ teaspoon ground black pepper

2 tablespoons sliced green onion, green part only

2 teaspoons lemon juice

1 Heat grill pan over medium heat.

2 Brush bread slices on both sides with 1 tablespoon olive oil. Add to grill pan and cook until toasted on both sides with distinct grill marks, about 2 minutes per side. Remove from grill pan and cut in half diagonally. Set aside.

3 In a 3-quart pot over medium heat, add remaining olive oil. Once hot, add garlic and cook 20 seconds, then stir in tomato and cook until just tender, about 1 minute.

4 Stir in wine and scrape any brown bits from bottom of pot. Add mussels and stir well. Cover pot with a lid and cook 5 minutes or until mussels have opened.

5 Remove lid and check that mussels have opened. Discard any that are still closed. Stir in cream, salt, and pepper and stir well. Add green onion and stir to combine.

6 Transfer to a serving bowl and drizzle with lemon juice. Place grilled bread against side of bowl. Serve immediately.

Ruby Tuesday New Orleans Seafood

SERVES 4

Known for their American cuisine, Ruby Tuesday features a large salad bar at their locations, along with pasta, steak, and burgers. This spicy fish and shrimp dish adds an American twist to Italian ingredients.

2½ pounds tilapia fillets

3 tablespoons olive oil

2 tablespoons Creole seasoning, plus more for dusting

1 cup Alfredo sauce

4 tablespoons salted butter

2 cloves garlic, minced

¾ pound shelled shrimp

3 tablespoons grated Parmesan cheese, for garnish

1 Preheat oven to 425°F.

2 Pat tilapia fillets dry with a paper towel. Brush fillets with olive oil and season with 2 tablespoons Creole seasoning on both sides.

3 Place in a well-greased half baking sheet and bake 10–12 minutes until cooked through and flesh flakes easily.

4 While fillets are baking, warm Alfredo sauce in a small pan.

5 In a 10-inch skillet over medium heat, melt butter. Add garlic and shrimp and sauté 5 minutes or until shrimp are cooked through and curled into a "C" shape.

6 Remove fillets from oven. Carefully place fillets on plates and top with a fourth of the cooked shrimp and ¼ cup Alfredo sauce each. Sprinkle with grated Parmesan cheese and a dusting of Creole seasoning. Serve immediately.

CHAPTER 8

Pasta and Noodle Entrées

Buca di Beppo Chicken Marsala

BUCA DI BEPPO

There are about eighty of these restaurants operating nationwide. The chain specializes in Italian American food, which is served family style and meant to be shared among the dining party.

Chicken Marsala is an elegant and delicious Italian dish that is also really easy to make. Food at Buca di Beppo is served family style, so serve this dish on a big platter in the center of the table.

4 (6-ounce) boneless, skinless chicken breasts

1 cup all-purpose flour

½ teaspoon salt

½ teaspoon ground black pepper

1 tablespoon dried oregano

2 tablespoons olive oil

1 tablespoon salted butter

2 cups marsala wine

3 cups chicken stock

1¼ cups sliced fresh baby portobello mushrooms

4 cloves garlic, minced

16 ounces dry linguine pasta, cooked per package directions

1 Place chicken breasts 1 at a time between two sheets of wax paper. Pound until chicken is about ¼-inch thick.

2 In a small bowl, combine flour, salt, pepper, and oregano. Dredge chicken in flour mixture until coated thoroughly.

3 Heat olive oil and butter in a 10-inch skillet over medium-high heat. Add chicken breasts and cook until almost fully cooked, about 3 minutes per side. Remove from pan and set aside.

4 Still over medium-high heat, add wine to pan, making sure to scrape any brown bits from bottom of pan. Add chicken stock, mushrooms, and garlic. Cook 10 minutes or until sauce has been reduced by half.

5 Return chicken to pan and cook 10 minutes more. Sauce should be thick. Place cooked pasta on a platter. Add chicken and pour sauce over top. Serve immediately.

Buca di Beppo Lasagna

Portions of lasagna at Buca di Beppo are known for their size! This copycat version has all the "towering" layers and all the flavor and makes an impressive dish for friends and family.

SERVES 8

1½ cups whole milk ricotta cheese

1 large egg, beaten

1 clove garlic, minced

Water, for boiling

1 tablespoon salt

1 (16-ounce) box dry lasagna noodles

8 ounces tomato sauce

16 ounces bulk sweet Italian sausage, cooked and crumbled

1 cup marinara sauce

2 cups shredded mozzarella cheese

½ cup grated Parmesan cheese

1 Preheat oven to 350°F and spray a 9-inch × 13-inch baking dish with nonstick cooking spray.

2 In a medium bowl, add ricotta, egg, and garlic. Mix until fully combined. Set aside.

3 In a 3-quart saucepan, add water, leaving a 3-inch gap at the top. Heat over high heat until water boils. Add salt and lasagna noodles and boil 12 minutes. Drain and rinse noodles with cold water.

4 In a medium bowl, combine tomato sauce and sausage. Set aside.

5 Add ½ cup marinara sauce to bottom of prepared dish. Add 4 noodles in an overlapping layer, spread ¾ cup ricotta mixture over noodles, and add ½ cup mozzarella. Add 4 noodles, spread 1 cup meat sauce over noodles, and sprinkle with ¼ cup Parmesan cheese. Add 4 noodles, spread ¾ cup ricotta mixture over noodles, and add ½ cup mozzarella. Add 4 noodles and 1 cup meat sauce. Add remaining noodles and spread remaining marinara sauce evenly over top.

6 Cover dish tightly with foil sprayed lightly with nonstick cooking spray. Bake 1 hour 20 minutes, then remove foil, top lasagna with remaining mozzarella and Parmesan cheeses, and return to oven 20 minutes or until cheeses are melted and golden brown.

7 Allow to rest 10 minutes before slicing and serving.

Buca di Beppo Spicy Chicken Rigatoni

SERVES 4

This creamy, spicy dish makes an impressive yet easy weekday meal. For variety you can use any tube-shaped pasta like ziti or macaroni or even a long pasta like fettuccine.

2 tablespoons olive oil

2 cloves garlic, minced

1 teaspoon crushed red pepper flakes

2 (6-ounce) boneless, skinless chicken breasts, cut into ½-inch strips

¼ teaspoon salt

¼ teaspoon ground black pepper

1 cup Alfredo sauce

2 cups marinara sauce

2 tablespoons salted butter

½ cup frozen peas

¼ cup heavy cream

16 ounces dry rigatoni pasta, cooked per package directions

¼ cup grated Parmesan cheese

1 In a 10-inch skillet over medium heat, add olive oil. Once hot, add garlic and red pepper flakes and cook 30 seconds. Add chicken, salt, and black pepper and cook, stirring constantly, until chicken is just cooked, about 5 minutes.

2 Add Alfredo sauce, marinara sauce, and butter and stir well. Once butter has melted, add peas and cream and stir to combine. Reduce heat to medium-low and simmer 3 minutes.

3 Add cooked pasta to pan and toss to combine. Serve immediately with Parmesan cheese for garnish.

Carrabba's Fettuccine Weesie

Fettuccine Weesie features seafood sautéed in lemon garlic butter mixed with creamy Alfredo sauce. This is a popular dish for seafood lovers for a reason!

3 tablespoons salted butter

2 cloves garlic, minced

1 tablespoon lemon juice

8 jumbo shrimp, peeled and deveined

1 tablespoon olive oil

¼ cup sliced button mushrooms

1 tablespoon sliced green onions

½ cup Alfredo sauce

8 ounces dry fettuccine pasta, cooked per package directions

½ cup grated Romano cheese

1 In a large saucepan over medium heat, add butter. Once melted, add garlic and sauté 30 seconds. Stir in lemon juice and mix well. Add shrimp and sauté 3–4 minutes until shrimp turn pink and curl into a "C" shape. Transfer to a medium bowl along with lemon butter and set aside.

2 Return pan to medium heat and add olive oil. Once hot, add mushrooms and let stand 3 minutes or until golden brown. Flip mushrooms and cook 3–5 minutes until golden brown. Add green onions and shrimp with lemon butter.

3 Stir Alfredo sauce into pan and cook 1 minute, then add cooked fettuccine and toss to coat.

4 Transfer to serving plates and garnish with Romano cheese. Serve immediately.

SERVES 2

ORIGIN OF FETTUCCINE ALFREDO

When fettuccine Alfredo was invented in Rome in the early 1900s, it contained only fresh noodles, butter, and Parmesan cheese. Americans added heavy cream to the recipe to make the fettuccine Alfredo served in US restaurants today.

Carrabba's Linguine Pescatore

SERVES 2

This dish features a variety of seafood in a spicy red sauce. You can use your favorite mix of shellfish and seafood here, so customize the mix to suit your taste.

2 tablespoons olive oil

1 clove garlic, minced

½ teaspoon crushed red pepper flakes

3 medium shrimp, peeled and deveined

3 medium scallops

6–8 mussels

1¼ cups marinara sauce

¼ teaspoon salt

¼ teaspoon ground white pepper

4 ounces dry linguine pasta, cooked per package directions

1 In a 10-inch skillet over medium heat, add olive oil. Once hot, add garlic and red pepper flakes and sauté 30 seconds.

2 Add all ingredients except linguine and cook 5 minutes until shrimp turns pink and mussels pop open.

3 Reduce heat to medium-low and add cooked linguine. Toss to evenly coat pasta. Cook 2 minutes to warm pasta and then serve.

The Cheesecake Factory Cajun Jambalaya Pasta

This is one of the California-based restaurant chains most popular dishes. While jambalaya is typically served over rice, this version features plump shrimp and chicken served over fresh-cooked linguine.

SERVES 4

½ cup salted butter

1 tablespoon Cajun seasoning

1 medium green bell pepper, seeded and julienned

1 medium red bell pepper, seeded and julienned

½ medium red onion, peeled and julienned

1 pound boneless, skinless chicken breasts, cut into 1-inch pieces

¼ cup seafood stock

½ pound medium shrimp, peeled and deveined

½ cup diced Roma tomatoes

16 ounces dry linguine pasta, cooked per package directions

½ teaspoon paprika

½ teaspoon dried parsley

1 In a large sauté pan, add butter and Cajun seasoning. Let butter melt until it starts to foam and seasoning become fragrant. Add peppers and onion and sauté 3 minutes. Add chicken and continue to cook 4 minutes or until chicken is about half done.

2 Pour seafood stock into pan and cook 1 minute or until chicken is almost done.

3 Add shrimp and toss ingredients together. Continue to cook 2 minutes, then add tomatoes and cook 5 minutes more or until both shrimp and chicken are thoroughly cooked.

4 Divide pasta between serving bowls. Spoon equal portions of jambalaya mixture over pasta. Garnish with paprika and parsley. Serve hot.

THE CHEESECAKE FACTORY CAJUN JAMBALAYA PASTA

Chili's Cajun Pasta

Serve up a spicy dinner with this hot and creamy penne tossed with chicken strips sautéed with Cajun seasoning. You can also make this dish with shrimp if you prefer.

SERVES 2

2 (6-ounce) boneless, skinless chicken breast halves, cut into strips

2 teaspoons Cajun seasoning

2 tablespoons salted butter

1½ cups heavy cream

¼ teaspoon dried basil

¼ teaspoon lemon pepper seasoning

¼ teaspoon salt

⅛ teaspoon ground black pepper

⅛ teaspoon garlic powder

4 ounces dry penne pasta, cooked per package directions

¼ cup grated Parmesan cheese

1 Place chicken and Cajun seasoning in a large resealable plastic bag. Rub and shake to coat chicken well.

2 In a 10-inch skillet over medium heat, melt butter. Add chicken and sauté about 5–7 minutes, then reduce heat to medium-low.

3 Add cream, basil, lemon pepper seasoning, salt, black pepper, and garlic powder. Stir 5 minutes or until sauce thickens.

4 Add pasta and toss. Heat 5 minutes more. Garnish with Parmesan cheese and serve.

Olive Garden Chicken Scampi

SERVES 4

Scampi is usually associated with shrimp, but at Olive Garden they also make it with chicken. Here it includes bell pepper and is served over angel hair pasta.

ROASTING GARLIC

To roast garlic: Separate a head of garlic into individual cloves still in the paper shell. Toss in olive oil, wrap tightly in foil, and bake in a 350°F oven for 45 minutes. When the garlic has cooled to the touch, you should be able to squeeze it out of each clove's shell.

4 tablespoons salted butter, divided

2 tablespoons all-purpose flour

¾ cup whole milk

2 tablespoons crushed garlic

2 teaspoons Italian seasoning

½ teaspoon crushed red pepper flakes

½ teaspoon ground black pepper

¾ cup dry white wine

1 cup chicken broth

1 tablespoon olive oil

2 (6-ounce) boneless, skinless chicken breasts, sliced into ½-inch strips

1 medium green bell pepper, seeded and thinly sliced

1 medium red onion, peeled and thinly sliced

10 cloves roasted garlic (see sidebar)

8 ounces dry angel hair pasta, cooked per package directions

1 Heat a 2-quart saucepan over medium heat. Add 1 tablespoon butter and once melted, add flour. Cook 2 minutes, stirring constantly. Slowly add milk and cook, stirring constantly, 3–4 minutes. Set aside.

2 Heat a 10-inch skillet over low heat and add remaining butter. Once melted, add crushed garlic, Italian seasoning, red pepper, and black pepper. Cook about 2 minutes. Add wine and chicken broth and stir until combined.

3 Add prepared white sauce to wine sauce and cook 5 minutes or until slightly thickened.

4 In a 10-inch skillet over high heat, add olive oil. Once hot, add chicken, bell pepper, and onion. Sauté 5 minutes or until chicken is cooked through and vegetables are tender.

5 Add thickened sauce and sauté until everything is warmed. Add roasted garlic cloves. Serve over hot pasta.

Panda Express Chow Mein

Chow mein is a Chinese American dish usually featuring bits of meat and vegetables served over noodles. If you are not able to find chow mein stir-fry noodles, you can swap them for lo mein or thin spaghetti.

SERVES 1

1 tablespoon vegetable oil

2 diced medium green onions

1½ cups sliced napa cabbage

¼ cup sliced celery

¼ cup bean sprouts

¼ teaspoon granulated sugar

½ cup chicken broth

½ tablespoon soy sauce

1 teaspoon sesame oil

½ tablespoon cornstarch dissolved in 1 tablespoon cold water

¼ teaspoon crushed red pepper flakes

4 ounces dry chow mein stir-fry noodles, cooked per package directions

1 In a medium cast iron skillet over medium heat, heat vegetable oil until hot but not smoking. Add green onions, cabbage, celery, and sprouts and stir-fry 3 minutes or until cabbage is wilted.

2 Reduce heat to medium-low and add sugar, broth, soy sauce, and sesame oil and allow to simmer 3 minutes.

3 Give dissolved cornstarch a stir and then stir into vegetable mixture. Increase heat to medium and bring liquid to a boil.

4 Add red pepper flakes. Reduce heat to low and simmer 5 minutes or until heated through. Serve over prepared noodles.

PANDA EXPRESS CHOW MEIN

P.F. Chang's Singapore Street Noodles

While this dish may not have any direct relation to Singapore, this popular menu item is a noodle dish. It features chicken and shrimp and P.F. Chang's signature curry sauce made with madras curry powder.

SERVES 4

2 tablespoons white vinegar

¼ cup madras curry powder

¼ cup light soy sauce

1 cup oyster sauce

¼ cup sriracha chili sauce

¼ cup ketchup

1 gallon water

1 pound rice stick noodles

4 tablespoons canola oil, divided

½ pound medium shrimp, peeled and deveined

8 ounces boneless, skinless chicken breast, thinly sliced

1 tablespoon chopped garlic

1 cup julienned cabbage

½ cup julienned carrots

2 medium tomatoes, diced

1 bunch green onions, sliced

⅓ cup diced shallots

¼ bunch cilantro, roughly chopped

Juice from 1 medium lime

1 teaspoon sesame oil

1 In a medium bowl, combine vinegar, curry powder, soy sauce, oyster sauce, chili sauce, and ketchup and mix well. Set aside.

2 In a large saucepan over high heat, bring water to a rolling boil. Add rice stick noodles and cook 2 minutes. Drain, then rinse under running hot water 1 minute and drain well again. Toss noodles with 2 tablespoons canola oil and set aside.

3 In a wok over high heat, add remaining canola oil. Once hot, add shrimp and chicken and stir-fry 2 minutes.

4 Add garlic, cabbage, carrots, and tomatoes and stir-fry 1 minute. Add cooked noodles and stir-fry 1 minute more.

5 Add 1 cup prepared sauce and stir-fry until ingredients are well incorporated, about 2 minutes.

6 Add green onions, shallots, cilantro, lime juice, and sesame oil and toss briefly. Serve.

Pizza Hut Oven-Baked Italian Meats Pasta

SERVES 4

Pizza Hut updated its pasta offerings in 2022 when they added a selection of oven-baked pasta dishes. This dish has all the flavor of a supreme pizza mixed with tender ziti pasta.

¼ cup salted butter

1 large yellow onion, peeled and diced

1 large green bell pepper, seeded and diced

1 teaspoon garlic powder

1 (16-ounce) jar marinara sauce

½ pound 80/20 ground beef, crumbled, browned, and drained

½ pound Italian sausage, crumbled, browned, and drained

16 ounces dry ziti pasta, cooked per package directions

½ pound thinly sliced pepperoni

½ cup sliced black olives

1 cup shredded mozzarella cheese

1 Preheat oven to 350°F.

2 In a 10-inch skillet over medium-high heat, add butter. Once melted, add onion, pepper, and garlic powder and sauté about 4 minutes.

3 In a medium saucepan, heat marinara and combine with beef and sausage.

4 Lightly grease a 13-inch × 11-inch baking dish with nonstick cooking spray. Place half of cooked pasta in dish, followed by half of vegetables, half of pepperoni, half of sauce, and half of black olives. Repeat to form a second layer.

5 Spread mozzarella cheese over top and bake 45 minutes or until cheese has melted and is lightly browned. Serve warm.

CHAPTER 9

Sides

Applebee's Garlic Mashed Potatoes

SERVES 8

An extremely popular side dish both at home and in restaurants, roasted garlic mashed potatoes are perfect served with grilled steak, chicken, or seafood. This version from Applebee's made with red potatoes is sure to be a hit at your table. It is not necessary to peel the potatoes unless you desire to.

4 cloves garlic

2 pounds red potatoes

½ cup whole milk

¼ cup heavy cream

3 tablespoons salted butter

½ teaspoon salt

½ teaspoon ground black pepper

1 Preheat oven to 400°F.

2 Place garlic cloves on a sheet of heavy-duty foil. Wrap garlic tightly in foil and roast 45 minutes or until soft. Unwrap garlic and let cool until touchable.

3 Place potatoes in a large pot of water over high heat. Bring to a boil and boil 20 minutes. Remove from heat and drain in a colander.

4 Peel garlic cloves. Combine garlic with potatoes and remaining ingredients and mash with a potato masher until smooth. Serve hot.

Bob Evans Bread & Celery Dressing

This bread dressing, made famous at the Bob Evans Restaurants, is perfect alongside roasted turkey or chicken dinners.

SERVES 6

16 ounces white bread, cubed

6 tablespoons unsalted butter

3 medium stalks celery, chopped

1 medium yellow onion, peeled and chopped

1 large carrot, chopped

1 teaspoon ground sage

1 teaspoon poultry seasoning

½ teaspoon salt

½ teaspoon ground black pepper

2 cups chicken stock

1 tablespoon dried parsley

1 Preheat oven to 200°F and line a half sheet pan with parchment.

2 Spread bread cubes on prepared sheet pan. Bake 20–25 minutes, stirring every 5 minutes, until bread is dry and crisp. Set aside to cool.

3 Increase oven temperature to 350°F and spray a 9-inch × 13-inch baking dish with nonstick cooking spray.

4 In a 10-inch skillet over medium heat, add butter. Once melted, add celery, onion, and carrot. Cook, stirring often, until tender, about 6 minutes. Remove from heat and stir in sage, poultry seasoning, salt, and pepper.

5 In a large bowl, add vegetable mixture and bread cubes. Fold to combine, then add chicken stock and stir until bread is moistened. Let stand 5 minutes to ensure bread is thoroughly saturated.

6 Transfer to prepared baking dish and spread evenly but do not compress. Sprinkle parsley over top. Bake 25–35 minutes until center of dressing is jiggly but edges are set. Cool 10 minutes before serving.

Buffalo Wild Wings Beer-Battered Onion Rings

SERVES 4

These onion rings make a delicious side dish for buffalo wings or hamburgers or as part of a party's appetizer buffet. Serve them fresh for the best flavor and texture.

Vegetable oil, for frying

1 cup all-purpose flour, divided

1 teaspoon salt

1 teaspoon paprika

½ teaspoon garlic powder

½ teaspoon onion powder

¾ cup lager-style beer

1 large yellow onion, peeled and cut into ½-inch rings

1 Fill deep fryer with oil per manufacturer directions and heat to 350°F, or in a 5½-quart Dutch oven add enough oil to fill pot by 3 inches, leaving at least 3 inches of space at the top, and place over medium-high heat until oil reaches 350°F.

2 In a medium bowl, combine ¾ cup flour, salt, paprika, garlic powder, and onion powder. Whisk to thoroughly combine, then whisk in beer until smooth.

3 In a separate bowl, combine onion rings and remaining flour. Toss to coat rings.

4 Dip rings 3 or 4 at a time in batter and then in hot oil. Fry 3–4 minutes until crisp and golden brown. Transfer to a paper towel lined–plate and repeat with remaining onion rings and batter. Serve hot.

Chick-fil-A Waffle Potato Fries

A mandoline slicer with the waffle (wavy) blade is needed to make the signature waffle shape for these popular fries. The potatoes are not peeled at Chick-fil-A, but you can peel them if you prefer.

4 large russet potatoes

Vegetable oil, for frying

1 teaspoon salt

1 Fill a large bowl with water. Set aside.

2 Cut potatoes in half widthwise. Fit mandoline with waffle blade. Slice cut side of 1 potato once, then turn 90 degrees and slice again to create a waffle-sliced potato. Check thickness and adjust until potato slices are approximately ¼-inch thick. Add potato slices to water to soak. Repeat until all potatoes are sliced, then let slices soak 30 minutes.

3 Fill deep fryer with oil per manufacturer directions and heat to 350°F, or in a 5½-quart Dutch oven add enough oil to fill pot by 3 inches, leaving at least 3 inches of space at the top, and place over medium-high heat until oil reaches 350°F.

4 Drain potato slices and dry thoroughly between layers of paper towels. Fry in batches in hot oil 3–4 minutes until golden brown. Transfer to a paper towel–lined plate and sprinkle lightly with salt. Repeat with remaining potato slices and salt. Serve hot.

Chipotle Cilantro Lime Rice

SERVES 2

Cilantro is a key herb in Mexican cooking, and this flavorful rice dish from Chipotle is great as a side dish alongside grilled chicken or fish, inside a burrito, or as a base for a burrito bowl.

1 teaspoon olive oil

2/3 cup white rice

1 medium lime, halved

1 cup water

1/2 teaspoon salt

2 teaspoons fresh chopped cilantro

1 In a 2-quart saucepan over low heat, add olive oil. Add rice and juice from half of lime. Sauté 1 minute.

2 Add water and salt. Increase heat to medium and bring to a boil. Once boiling, cover and reduce heat to low and cook until rice is tender and water is absorbed, about 25 minutes.

3 Remove rice from heat and add cilantro and juice from remaining half of lime. Cover and let rice stand 10 minutes, then fluff rice with a fork and serve hot.

Cracker Barrel Carrots

SERVES 4

These glazed baby carrots from Cracker Barrel make a nice side dish for almost any meal, but are exceptionally good with steak, beef roast, or chicken. They also make an easy and flavorful holiday side dish.

1/4 cup salted butter

1 (1-pound) package washed baby carrots

2 tablespoons water

2 tablespoons packed light brown sugar

1/4 teaspoon salt

1 In a 2-quart saucepan over medium heat, add butter. Once melted, add remaining ingredients and stir well.

2 Cover pan and reduce heat to medium-low. Cook 35–40 minutes, stirring every 10 minutes. Serve hot.

Cracker Barrel Cornbread Dressing

This Southern-style stuffing is a holiday favorite at Cracker Barrel restaurants where it is served along with roast turkey and gravy. It will be sure to be a hit at your holiday table too.

SERVES 16

⅔ cup chopped yellow onion

2 cups chopped celery

8 cups crumbled day-old cornbread

4 cups grated day-old biscuits

¼ cup dried parsley

2 teaspoons poultry seasoning

2 teaspoons ground sage

1 teaspoon ground black pepper

½ cup salted butter, melted

1 quart plus 1 (14-ounce) can chicken broth

1 large egg, beaten

1 Preheat oven to 400°F and spray two 8-inch cake pans with non-stick cooking spray.

2 In a large mixing bowl, mix onion, celery, cornbread, biscuits, parsley, poultry seasoning, sage, and pepper. Add butter and blend well.

3 Add chicken broth and egg and mix well. Mixture should have a wet but not soupy consistency, like pancake batter.

4 Divide mixture evenly between prepared cake pans. Bake uncovered 1 hour or until lightly browned on top. Serve.

Cracker Barrel Corn Muffins

SERVES 12

These sweet and savory muffins are just like the ones served before your meal at Cracker Barrel and are perfect with a smear of butter and drizzle of honey.

CRACKER BARREL AT HOME

Cracker Barrel is so popular they introduced a line of mixes for their pancakes, biscuits, and corn muffins you can buy in their country stores. You can also buy their fried apples, pancake syrup, and apple butter.

1 cup white cornmeal

1 cup all-purpose flour

¼ cup granulated sugar

1 tablespoon baking powder

½ teaspoon salt

¼ teaspoon baking soda

1 cup low-fat buttermilk

¼ cup unsalted butter, melted

2 tablespoons vegetable oil

1 large egg, beaten

1 Preheat oven to 400°F and spray a 12-cup muffin pan with nonstick cooking spray.

2 In a large mixing bowl, sift together cornmeal, flour, sugar, baking powder, salt, and baking soda. Make a well in center and set aside.

3 In a medium bowl, combine buttermilk, butter, oil, and egg. Whisk until smooth.

4 Pour buttermilk mixture into well in dry ingredients. Mix until just combined and no large lumps remain. (Small lumps are okay.)

5 Divide batter evenly between prepared muffin cups. Bake 14–18 minutes until muffins spring back when gently pressed in center. Cool 5 minutes in pan, then turn out into a basket lined with a clean towel and cover with a second towel. Enjoy warm.

Cracker Barrel Green Beans

These country-style green beans are flavored just the way you like them at Cracker Barrel, with bacon and pepper.

SERVES 8

¼ pound sliced bacon, chopped

3 (14.5-ounce) cans whole green beans

½ teaspoon salt

1 teaspoon granulated sugar

1 teaspoon ground black pepper

¼ medium yellow onion, peeled and diced

1 In a 2-quart saucepan over medium heat, add bacon and cook 6–8 minutes until lightly browned but not crisp.
2 Add green beans, including liquid from cans. Add salt, sugar, and pepper and mix well.
3 Place onion over top of green beans. Cover pan and bring to a boil. Reduce heat to low and simmer 40–45 minutes until beans are very tender. Serve hot.

Cracker Barrel Mmmm Mac N' Cheese

SERVES 6

Macaroni and cheese is always a family favorite, and this savory and creamy version from Cracker Barrel will be sure to please everyone in your family with its golden brown topping.

2 cups dry elbow pasta
¼ cup salted butter
¼ cup all-purpose flour
1 cup chicken broth
1½ cups whole milk
½ cup cubed deli American cheese
2½ cups shredded colby jack cheese, divided

1 Preheat broiler to 500°F and spray a 2-quart casserole dish with nonstick cooking spray.
2 Cook pasta according to instructions, drain, and set aside.
3 In a 2-quart saucepan over medium heat, add butter and once melted and foaming, add flour. Cook, stirring constantly, 1 minute. Whisk in broth and milk. Bring mixture to a simmer over medium heat, about 5 minutes.
4 Reduce heat to low and whisk in American cheese. Once melted, add 2 cups colby jack cheese and whisk until smooth. Fold in cooked pasta.
5 Transfer to prepared casserole dish and top with remaining colby jack cheese. Broil 3–4 minutes until cheese topping is melted and deeply golden brown. Cool 2 minutes before serving.

CRACKER BARREL MMMM MAC N' CHEESE

KFC Cole Slaw

SERVES 10

What is it about that tasty KFC Cole Slaw that makes you want to go back for more? Now you can make it at home with this recipe.

⅓ cup granulated sugar

½ teaspoon salt

⅛ teaspoon ground black pepper

¼ cup whole milk

½ cup mayonnaise

¼ cup low-fat buttermilk

1½ tablespoons white vinegar

2½ tablespoons lemon juice

1 medium head cabbage, finely chopped

1 medium carrot, finely chopped

2 tablespoons minced yellow onion

1 In a large bowl, combine sugar, salt, pepper, milk, mayonnaise, buttermilk, vinegar, and lemon juice and beat until smooth.

2 Add cabbage, carrot, and onion and mix well.

3 Cover and refrigerate at least 2 hours before serving.

KFC Mashed Potatoes and Gravy

Mashed Potatoes and Gravy is an immensely popular side item on the KFC menu. The gravy has a deliciously distinct taste that now you can replicate at home with this recipe.

SERVES 4

Mashed Potatoes

2½ cups hot water

2 tablespoons salted butter

½ cup margarine

1 teaspoon salt

2½ cups Idahoan potato flakes

¾ cup whole milk

Gravy

1½ tablespoons melted shortening

3 tablespoons bread flour, divided

2 tablespoons all-purpose flour

1 (10-ounce) can condensed chicken stock

1¼ cups water

¼ teaspoon salt

⅛ teaspoon Accent Flavor Enhancer

⅛ teaspoon ground black pepper

2 chicken bouillon cubes

1 (10-ounce) jar Franco American Beef Gravy

1/16 teaspoon ground sage

1 For the mashed potatoes: In a 2-quart pot over high heat, add water, butter, and margarine. Once melted, add salt and bring to a boil, about 2 minutes. Add potato flakes and mix until flakes start to resemble mashed potatoes. Reduce heat to medium-low and add milk 2–3 tablespoons at a time to reach desired consistency. Remove from heat.

2 For the gravy: Heat a 1-quart saucepan over medium-low heat. Add shortening and 1½ tablespoons bread flour. Cook, stirring constantly, for 5 minutes or until mixture browns in color to resemble milk chocolate.

3 Remove from heat and add remaining bread flour and all-purpose flour. Slowly whisk in chicken stock, water, salt, Accent Flavor Enhancer, pepper, bouillon cubes, beef gravy, and sage so no lumps remain.

4 Return to stove and bring to a boil over medium heat and boil 2 minutes. Reduce heat to medium-low and allow gravy to thicken, about 3–5 minutes until it reaches desired consistency. Serve over mashed potatoes.

KFC Secret Recipe Fries

SERVES 8

Frying these fries twice adds a deeper crisp to the outer coating and ensures the insides of the fries will be tender and fluffy. Leftover fries can be reheated in a 350°F oven or an air fryer for 5–8 minutes.

1 cup whole milk

1 large egg

1 cup all-purpose flour

1 teaspoon salt

½ teaspoon ground black pepper

½ teaspoon paprika

½ teaspoon garlic powder

4 large russet potatoes

Vegetable oil, for frying

1 In a medium bowl, add milk and egg and whisk to combine.

2 In a separate medium bowl, add flour, salt, pepper, paprika, and garlic powder and whisk to combine.

3 Cut potatoes into ¼-inch square fries. Add to milk mixture and let stand for 20 minutes.

4 Fill deep fryer with oil per manufacturer directions and heat to 325°F, or in a 5½-quart Dutch oven add enough oil to fill pot by 3 inches, leaving at least 3 inches of space at the top, and place over medium-high heat until oil reaches 325°F.

5 Remove six to eight fries from milk mixture and drain well. Add to seasoned flour and toss to coat.

6 Fry fries in hot oil 5 minutes or until lightly browned and tender. Transfer to a paper towel lined–plate and repeat with remaining potato wedges and seasoned flour.

7 Increase oil temperature to 350°F. Return fries to oil in batches and fry 2–3 minutes or until very crisp and deeply golden. Serve immediately.

KFC Sweet Corn

This version of the popular KFC side is coated in seasoned butter to add a savory edge. If you can't find super sweet corn, use regular cut corn and add an extra teaspoon of sugar.

SERVES 6

½ cup unsalted butter, softened

16 ounces frozen super sweet corn kernels

1 teaspoon fresh lemon juice

½ teaspoon salt

½ teaspoon granulated sugar

¼ teaspoon ground black pepper

¼ teaspoon garlic powder

In a 2-quart saucepan over medium heat, add butter. Once melted, add remaining ingredients and cook, stirring often, until corn is steaming hot, about 8 minutes. Serve hot.

LongHorn Steakhouse Crispy Brussels Sprouts

SERVES 2

Most people think potatoes when they think steakhouse, but at LongHorn Steakhouse one of the most popular sides are these crispy Brussels sprouts drizzled with a spicy-sweet glaze!

1 pound Brussels sprouts, ends trimmed

2 teaspoons salt

2 tablespoons olive oil

2 tablespoons salted butter, melted

1 tablespoon honey

1 teaspoon crushed red pepper flakes

½ teaspoon smoked paprika

½ teaspoon chili powder

1 Preheat oven to 400°F and line a half sheet pan with foil sprayed with nonstick cooking spray.

2 Fill a large pot with water. Bring to a boil over high heat and add Brussels sprouts and salt. Boil 5 minutes or until tender. Drain and rinse well with cold water.

3 Cut sprouts in half and add to a large bowl. Add olive oil and toss to coat. Place sprouts on prepared baking sheet cut side down. Bake 20–25 minutes, stirring halfway through cooking time, until golden brown and crispy.

4 While sprouts bake, combine butter, honey, red pepper flakes, paprika, and chili powder in a small bowl and mix well.

5 Remove sprouts from oven and transfer to a serving plate. Drizzle with sauce and toss gently to coat. Serve hot.

LONGHORN STEAKHOUSE CRISPY BRUSSELS SPROUTS

Outback Steakhouse Aussie Cheese Fries

These cheese fries make a great side dish or appetizer, and their steak seasoning gives them a rich, savory flavor. Outback Steakhouse also serves these without the cheese and toppings, so feel free to serve as you prefer.

Vegetable oil, for frying

1 pound frozen French fries

1 teaspoon steak seasoning

½ cup shredded Cheddar cheese

½ cup shredded Monterey jack cheese

6 strips bacon, cooked and crumbled

1 Preheat oven to 350°F. Line a half baking sheet with parchment.
2 Fill deep fryer with oil per manufacturer directions and heat to 350°F, or in a 5½-quart Dutch oven add enough oil to fill pot by 3 inches, leaving at least 3 inches of space at the top, and place over medium-high heat until oil reaches 350°F.
3 Fry French fries in hot oil in small batches according to package directions. Drain fries on a paper towel lined–plate and season with steak seasoning.
4 Place cooked fries on prepared baking sheet and top with cheeses and bacon. Bake 10 minutes or until cheeses melt. Serve immediately.

Outback Steakhouse Sweet Potato

A baked sweet potato loaded with butter, honey, and cinnamon is a delicious alternative to the ordinary spuds served at most steakhouses. You can save some time at home by using prepared honey butter from the grocery store.

SERVES 1

1 large sweet potato

1 tablespoon olive oil

1 tablespoon salt

3 tablespoons unsalted butter, softened

3 tablespoons honey

1 teaspoon ground cinnamon

1 Preheat oven to 350°F.

2 Rub outside of potato with olive oil and sprinkle with salt.

3 Bake potato directly on oven rack 45–60 minutes until a paring knife can be inserted easily into potato. Remove from oven and place on a serving plate.

4 Split potato in half lengthwise.

5 In a small bowl, whip together butter and honey and then smear on each potato half. Sprinkle cinnamon over top of honey butter. Serve immediately.

Panda Express Fried Rice

Fried Rice is a popular side dish at Panda Express that can be served with any of their main dishes, but it also makes a good main dish for meat-free days. For the best texture use leftover cooked rice.

1 tablespoon vegetable oil, divided

¼ cup chopped green onion, white part only

¼ cup frozen peas and carrots

2 large eggs, beaten

2 cups cooked and cooled white rice

1 tablespoon light soy sauce

1 teaspoon sesame oil

¼ cup thinly sliced green onion, green part only

1 In a 10-inch skillet over medium-high heat, add 1 teaspoon vegetable oil. Once hot, swirl to coat bottom of pan and add chopped green onion and frozen peas and carrots. Cook 30 seconds or until peas and carrots are thawed. Transfer to a plate and set aside.

2 Return pan to medium-high heat and add remaining vegetable oil. Once hot, swirl to coat bottom of pan and add eggs. Let eggs stand 10 seconds, then scramble 30 seconds. Add rice, breaking up any large clumps, and mix with eggs.

3 Fold in cooked vegetables, soy sauce, sesame oil, and sliced green onion. Mix until fully combined and hot, about 1 minute. Serve hot.

Panera Bread Mac & Cheese

Cozy, creamy, and loaded with cheesy flavor, Panera Bread's Mac & Cheese is popular for a reason. You can also add 1 cup chopped cooked broccoli or six strips of cooked and crumbled bacon for some variety!

SERVES 4

3 cups water

8 ounces dry medium shell pasta

1 tablespoon salt, divided

2 tablespoons unsalted butter

2 tablespoons all-purpose flour

¾ cup whole milk

¾ cup heavy cream

¼ cup cubed white American cheese

1¼ cups shredded sharp white Cheddar cheese

½ teaspoon ground black pepper

¼ teaspoon mustard powder

1　In a 2-quart pot over high heat, add water and bring to a boil. Once boiling, add pasta and 2 teaspoons salt. Cook pasta according to package directions, drain, and set aside.

2　Return pot to stove over medium heat and add butter. Once melted, add flour and whisk 1 minute. Slowly whisk in milk and cream. Continue whisking while mixture comes to a boil and thickens, about 3 minutes.

3　Reduce heat to low and whisk in American cheese. Once thoroughly melted, add in remaining salt, Cheddar, pepper, and mustard powder. Whisk until smooth.

4　Remove sauce from heat and fold in pasta. Serve immediately.

Popeyes Biscuits

SERVES 9
(YIELDS 18 BISCUITS)

POPEYES

The Popeyes franchise began in Louisiana in the early 1970s. They serve chicken products in mild and spicy flavors and offer sides such as Cajun Fries, Mashed Potatoes with Cajun Gravy, and Homestyle Mac & Cheese.

Any good Southern meal should include some biscuits, and this recipe from Popeyes makes a big batch that can be frozen. The secret to their signature buttery flavor is to brush them with butter before and after baking.

4 cups Bisquick Original Pancake & Baking Mix

8 ounces sour cream

¾ cup club soda

¼ cup salted butter, melted

1 Preheat oven to 400°F and line a half baking sheet with parchment.

2 In a large bowl, mix together Bisquick, sour cream, and club soda. Turn dough out onto lightly floured wax paper and pat dough into ½-inch flat rectangle with your hand. Cut with a 2-inch biscuit cutter into eighteen biscuits.

3 Place biscuits on prepared baking sheet. Brush half of melted butter over biscuits, then bake 15–20 minutes.

4 Brush remaining butter over biscuits as soon as they come out of oven. Serve warm.

Popeyes Red Beans & Rice

Famed New Orleans restauranteur and chef, the late Warren Leruth, also worked as a consultant for many popular restaurant chains. The original Red Beans & Rice recipe for Popeyes was created by him!

1 (16-ounce) can red chili beans in chili gravy

1 teaspoon chili powder

¼ teaspoon ground cumin

⅛ teaspoon garlic salt

2 cups cooked long-grain rice

1 In a 2-quart saucepan over medium-low heat, add beans. Heat beans without letting boil. Stir in chili powder, cumin, and garlic salt. Cook 5 minutes or until steaming hot but not boiling.

2 Add cooked rice and gently mix. Serve hot.

RED BEANS AND RICE

Red beans and rice originated in Louisiana and was traditionally made on Mondays, which was washday. Leftover meat from Sunday dinner such as pork, ham, or sausage was added to a big pot of beans along with vegetables and spices and slow cooked. This allowed homemakers to do the laundry and still have dinner ready to serve over rice.

Red Lobster Cheddar Bay Biscuits

**SERVES 6
(YIELDS 12 BISCUITS)**

For many people, the Cheddar Bay Biscuits at Red Lobster are more popular than the seafood dishes. They were created in 1992 by Kurt Hankins, and by 2017 the restaurants were selling nearly one million biscuits per day!

2 cups Bisquick Original Pancake & Baking Mix

⅔ cup whole milk

½ cup finely shredded Cheddar cheese

½ cup salted butter, melted

¼ teaspoon garlic powder

¼ teaspoon dried parsley

1 Preheat oven to 450°F and line a half sheet pan with parchment.
2 In a large bowl, mix Bisquick, milk, and cheese until a soft dough forms. Drop twelve mounds onto prepared baking sheet.
3 Bake 10–12 minutes until golden brown.
4 While biscuits bake, mix butter and garlic powder in a small bowl. Set aside.
5 Brush butter mixture over biscuits just after they come out of the oven and sprinkle tops with parsley. Cool 5 minutes before serving.

RED LOBSTER CHEDDAR BAY BISCUITS

Red Robin Garlic Fries

SERVES 4

In 1994, Red Robin started their bottomless steak fries promotion and it was an instant hit. They now have a Bottomless menu that includes Garlic Fries, Sweet Potato Fries, Coleslaw, and Steamed Broccoli!

12 ounces frozen steak cut fries

⅓ cup grated Parmesan cheese, divided

2 tablespoons salted butter

½ teaspoon garlic powder

¼ teaspoon ground black pepper

1 Preheat oven to 450°F and line a half sheet pan with parchment.

2 Spread fries on prepared sheet pan and bake 20 minutes or until sizzling and golden brown.

3 While fries bake, combine 3 tablespoons Parmesan cheese, butter, garlic powder, and pepper in a medium bowl and mix well.

4 Remove fries from oven and let stand 3 minutes, then transfer to bowl and toss in seasoned butter. Transfer to a serving plate and sprinkle with remaining Parmesan cheese. Serve immediately.

CHAPTER 10

Desserts

Arby's Apple Turnovers

SERVES 8

Aside from milkshakes, turnovers are the bestselling dessert at Arby's. This recipe is easier than apple pie, and you get the same great taste as the restaurant favorite without all the work.

4 large cooking apples, peeled, cored, and sliced

½ cup granulated sugar

1 tablespoon cornstarch

1 teaspoon lemon juice

¼ teaspoon ground cinnamon

1 (17.3-ounce) package puff pastry sheets

½ cup confectioners' sugar

1 tablespoon water

1 In a medium saucepan over low heat, cook apples with granulated sugar, cornstarch, lemon juice, and cinnamon, stirring frequently, 6–8 minutes until apples are tender. Refrigerate until chilled, about 2 hours.

2 Thaw puff pastry sheets at room temperature 20 minutes.

3 Preheat oven to 400°F.

4 Unfold pastry on a lightly floured surface. Roll each sheet into a 12-inch square, then cut into four 6-inch squares. Place ¼ cup apple mixture in center of each square. Brush edges with water. Fold to form triangles and seal edges firmly with a fork.

5 Place on half baking sheets and bake 25 minutes or until golden. Cool on a wire rack.

6 In a small bowl, mix together confectioners' sugar and water. With a spoon, drizzle sugar drizzle over turnovers and allow to set before serving.

Bob Evans Reese's Peanut Butter Pie

This no-bake pie is a winner for peanut better lovers, and one of the most popular pies at Bob Evans. This is also a great pie to make in the warmer months since you do not need to heat your oven.

1 (5-ounce) package Jell-O Vanilla Instant Pudding and Pie Filling Mix

2 cups cold whole milk

½ cup whipped cream

1¼ cups creamy peanut butter

1 (9-inch) prepared chocolate cookie crust, such as Keebler Ready Crust

1 (8-ounce) container Cool Whip

2 tablespoons chocolate syrup

2 tablespoons crushed peanuts

1 In a large bowl, whisk together pudding mix and milk until creamy. Add whipped cream and peanut butter and whisk until completely blended.

2 Pour into pie crust and cover with a generous layer of Cool Whip. Place in freezer 1 hour or until set.

3 Remove from freezer and drizzle with chocolate syrup and crushed peanuts.

4 Cover and chill 2 hours. Serve.

The Cheesecake Factory
Fresh Strawberry Cheesecake

SERVES 8

The Cheesecake Factory Bakery opened in 1972, and in 1978 the owners' son opened the first restaurant as a way to feature his mother, Evelyn Overton's, scrumptious cheesecakes. Today The Cheesecake Factory is known for cheesecakes and delicious food.

¼ cup unsalted butter, melted

1¼ cups granulated sugar, divided

1½ cups graham cracker crumbs

1½ pounds cream cheese, room temperature

5 large eggs, room temperature

1 cup sour cream, room temperature

¼ cup all-purpose flour

2 teaspoons pure vanilla extract

¼ teaspoon salt

4 cups fresh strawberries, hulled

1 (12-ounce) container glaze for strawberries

2 cups whipped cream

1 Preheat oven to 375°F.

2 In a large bowl, combine butter, ¼ cup sugar, and graham cracker crumbs and press ⅔ of mixture evenly onto bottom of a greased 10-inch springform pan. Use remaining mixture to press halfway up sides of pan. Use a measuring cup or glass with straight sides and bottom to compact mixture into an even thickness.

3 Bake crust for 10 minutes, then remove from oven and cool to room temperature, about 30 minutes.

4 Beat cream cheese with an electric mixer until light and fluffy. Add in remaining sugar, then eggs. Stir in sour cream, flour, vanilla, and salt until combined.

5 Pour mixture over baked crust. Wrap bottom of pan tightly with foil. Place in a 16-inch roasting pan and fill pan with recently boiled water until it reaches halfway up the side of the pan. Carefully transfer to oven and bake for 10 minutes, then reduce heat to 325°F and bake for another 60–70 minutes, or until edges of cheesecake are set but center is still slightly wobbly when shaken.

6 Turn off oven and let stand for 40 minutes, then prop door open several inches and allow cheesecake to rest in oven 1 hour. Remove cheesecake from water bath, discard foil, and cool to room temperature, about 1 hour, then cover and refrigerate overnight.

7 To serve, gently run a paring knife around edge of springform pan and release ring. Place cheesecake slices on dessert plates. Dip 2–3 strawberries into glaze and place on each plate. Garnish with whipped cream. Serve immediately.

The Cheesecake Factory Pumpkin Cheesecake

SERVES 8

THE CHEESECAKE FACTORY

The Cheesecake Factory has over 300 restaurants and boasts more than 200 items on the menu. There are over thirty different cheesecake varieties on their website, available for pickup or delivery.

While The Cheesecake Factory is famous for all kinds of cheesecakes, this seasonal cheesecake is always highly anticipated by pumpkin spice lovers. It is so popular its return often makes the news!

1½ cups graham cracker crumbs

5 tablespoons unsalted butter, melted

1 cup plus 1 tablespoon granulated sugar, divided

3 (8-ounce) softened packages cream cheese

1 teaspoon pure vanilla extract

1 cup canned pumpkin

3 large eggs

½ teaspoon ground cinnamon

¼ teaspoon ground nutmeg

¼ teaspoon allspice

Whipped cream, for topping

1 Preheat oven to 350°F.

2 In a medium bowl, combine graham cracker crumbs, butter, and 1 tablespoon sugar. Stir well enough to coat all crumbs with butter.

3 Press crumbs onto bottom and about two-thirds of the way up sides of an ungreased 9-inch pie pan. Bake crust 5 minutes. Set aside.

4 In a large mixing bowl, combine cream cheese, remaining sugar, and vanilla. Mix with an electric mixer until smooth.

5 Add pumpkin, eggs, cinnamon, nutmeg, and allspice and continue to beat until smooth and creamy.

6 Pour filling over crust. Bake 60–70 minutes until top of filling darkens a bit. Remove from oven and allow cheesecake to cool.

7 Once cheesecake has come to room temperature, place in refrigerator.

8 Serve with a generous portion of whipped cream on top.

Chili's Molten Chocolate Cakes

Molten Chocolate Cake is the most popular dessert on the Chili's menu. They serve this cake topped with a scoop of vanilla ice cream coated in a crunchy chocolate shell that can be made easily at home with Smucker's Magic Shell Chocolate Flavored Topping.

SERVES 4

5 tablespoons unsalted butter, plus more for greasing

2 teaspoons cocoa powder, plus more for dusting

3½ ounces dark chocolate, chopped

2 large eggs

1 large egg yolk

3 teaspoons granulated sugar

1 teaspoon pure vanilla extract

3 tablespoons all-purpose flour

1 teaspoon salt

1 Grease four 5-ounce ramekins with butter and dust with cocoa powder.

2 In a medium microwave-safe bowl, melt 5 tablespoons butter and chocolate together in microwave on medium heat 2–3 minutes. Stir to combine.

3 In a large mixing bowl, whisk together eggs, egg yolk, sugar, and vanilla until mixture is light yellow in color and sugar is dissolved.

4 Stir chocolate mixture into egg mixture and whisk until combined. Sift in flour, 2 teaspoons cocoa powder, and salt, then fold in with a spatula until combined.

5 Spoon batter into buttered ramekins and tap on table to settle any air bubbles. Refrigerate 30 minutes.

6 Preheat oven to 425°F.

7 Place ramekins in a 9" × 13" baking dish and add water to dish until halfway up sides of ramekins. Bake 15 minutes.

8 Run a knife blade around the sides of ramekins to loosen cakes. Place a serving dish on top of each ramekin and then flip over to release cake onto dish. Serve warm.

ORIGINS OF THE LAVA CAKE

Legend has it that this cake was the result of a major culinary disaster. A cook took chocolate sponge cakes out of the oven too soon, leaving the centers still liquefied. Since there was no time to cook the cakes further, the chef simply introduced the dessert as a chocolate lava cake.

Crumbl Birthday Cake Cookies

SERVES 8

At Crumbl you can get a free cookie on your birthday if you sign up for their Crumbl Loyalty program. Since their flavors are rotating, you may not be able to get a Birthday Cake Cookie in the store, so make a batch of these to celebrate!

Cookies

¾ cup unsalted butter, room temperature

¾ cup granulated sugar

1 large egg

1 large egg white

1 teaspoon pure vanilla extract

¼ teaspoon almond extract

¼ teaspoon butter extract

2 cups all-purpose flour

1 teaspoon cornstarch

1½ teaspoons baking powder

¼ teaspoon salt

1 cup rainbow sprinkles

Frosting and Topping

4 ounces cream cheese, room temperature

2 tablespoons unsalted butter, room temperature

¼ teaspoon pure vanilla extract

⅛ teaspoon almond extract

⅛ teaspoon butter extract

2 cups confectioners' sugar

1 tablespoon rainbow sprinkles

1 For the cookies: In work bowl of a stand mixer fitted with paddle attachment or in a large bowl with a hand mixer, add butter. Cream 30 seconds on low speed until creamy. Add granulated sugar and beat 3 minutes on medium speed or until fluffy. Add egg and egg white and beat on medium speed 1 minute, then stir in vanilla extract, almond extract, and butter extract.

2 In a medium bowl, sift together flour, cornstarch, baking powder, and salt. Add dry ingredients to wet ingredients and beat on low speed until just combined, then fold in sprinkles.

3 Cover dough with plastic wrap and refrigerate 2 hours or overnight.

4 Preheat oven to 350°F and line a half baking sheet with parchment.

5 Divide dough into eight equal pieces. Roll each piece into a ball. Place four balls on prepared baking sheet 2 inches apart. Bake 10–12 minutes until cookies are set and no longer shiny. Remove from oven and cool on baking sheet 10 minutes before transferring to a wire rack to cool completely. Repeat with remaining dough balls.

6 For the frosting and topping: In work bowl of a stand mixer fitted with paddle attachment or in a large bowl with a hand mixer, add cream cheese and butter. Beat 1 minute on low speed to combine. Add remaining ingredients except sprinkles and mix on low speed 30 seconds, then increase to medium and beat 1 minute.

7 When cookies have cooled completely, load frosting into a piping bag fitted with a round tip. Pipe frosting in a swirl over cookies and top with sprinkles. Enjoy at room temperature or chilled.

Crumbl Classic Pink Sugar Cookies

SERVES 8

Crumbl opened their first retail location in 2017 in Utah and quickly became a hit. The Classic Pink Sugar Cookie with its bright pink almond-flavored frosting is one of the cookies most associated with the brand.

Cookies

¾ cup unsalted butter, room temperature

¾ cup granulated sugar

1 large egg

1 large egg white

1 teaspoon pure vanilla extract

¼ teaspoon almond extract

2 cups all-purpose flour

1 teaspoon cornstarch

1½ teaspoons baking powder

Frosting

¼ cup unsalted butter, room temperature

¼ cup vegetable shortening

3 cups confectioners' sugar

½ teaspoon pure vanilla extract

½ teaspoon almond extract

2 tablespoons whole milk

¼ teaspoon rose pink gel food coloring

1 For the cookies: In work bowl of a stand mixer fitted with paddle attachment or in a large bowl with a hand mixer, add butter. Beat 30 seconds on low speed until creamy. Add granulated sugar and beat 3 minutes on medium speed or until fluffy. Add egg and egg white and beat on medium speed 1 minute, then stir in vanilla extract and almond extract.

2 In a medium bowl, sift together flour, cornstarch, and baking powder. Add dry ingredients to wet ingredients and beat on low speed until just combined, about 20 seconds.

3 Cover dough with plastic wrap and refrigerate 2 hours or overnight.

4 Preheat oven to 350°F and line a half baking sheet with parchment.

5 Divide dough into eight equal pieces. Roll each piece into a ball. Place four balls on prepared baking sheet 2 inches apart. Bake 12–15 minutes until cookies are set and no longer shiny. Remove from oven and cool on baking sheet 10 minutes before

transferring to a wire rack to cool completely. Repeat with remaining cookie dough.

6 For the frosting: In work bowl of a stand mixer fitted with paddle attachment or in a large bowl with a hand mixer, add butter and shortening. Beat 1 minute on low speed to combine. Add confectioners' sugar, vanilla extract, almond extract, and 1 tablespoon milk. Mix on low speed 30 seconds, then increase speed to medium and beat 1 minute more. If mixture seems too dry, add remaining milk. Add food coloring and mix on low to combine evenly, about 30 seconds.

7 When cookies have cooled, spread frosting over cookies in a thick layer. Enjoy at room temperature or chilled.

CRUMBL CLASSIC PINK SUGAR COOKIES

Crumbl Milk Chocolate Chip Cookies

This version of the popular Crumbl Chocolate Chip Cookie uses milk chocolate chips to give them a mild chocolaty flavor. To get the closest to Crumbl flavor, use Guittard chocolate.

SERVES 8

¾ cup unsalted butter, room temperature

¾ cup packed light brown sugar

⅓ cup granulated sugar

1 large egg, room temperature

1 teaspoon pure vanilla extract

2 cups all-purpose flour

2 teaspoons cornstarch

1 teaspoon baking soda

½ teaspoon baking powder

¼ teaspoon salt

1½ cups milk chocolate chips

1 In work bowl of a stand mixer fitted with paddle attachment or in a large bowl with a hand mixer, add butter. Cream 30 seconds on low speed until creamy. Add brown sugar and granulated sugar and beat 3 minutes on medium speed or until fluffy. Add egg and beat on medium speed 1 minute. Stir in vanilla.

2 In a medium bowl sift together flour, cornstarch, baking soda, and baking powder. Add flour mixture and salt to work bowl or large bowl and beat on low speed until just combined, about 30 seconds. Fold in chocolate chips with a spatula to combine.

3 Cover dough with plastic wrap and refrigerate 2 hours or overnight.

4 Preheat oven to 375°F and line a half baking sheet with parchment.

5 Divide dough into eight equal pieces. Roll each piece into a ball and lightly flatten. Place four balls on prepared baking sheet 2 inches apart. Bake 15–18 minutes, then remove from oven and cool on baking sheet 10 minutes before transferring to a wire rack to cool completely. Repeat with remaining cookie dough. Enjoy warm or at room temperature.

Crumbl Ultimate Peanut Butter Cookies

SERVES 8

You can dress these cookies up a bit by topping them with a smear of creamy peanut butter and a sprinkle of chopped peanut butter cups. You can also fold 3/4 cup peanut butter chips in the batter for more texture and peanut butter flavor.

½ cup creamy peanut butter

⅓ cup unsalted butter, room temperature

⅔ cup packed light brown sugar

3 tablespoons granulated sugar

1 large egg, room temperature

1 teaspoon pure vanilla extract

1¼ cups all-purpose flour

½ teaspoon baking soda

¼ teaspoon salt

1 In work bowl of a stand mixer fitted with paddle attachment or in a medium bowl with a hand mixer, combine peanut butter and butter. Beat on low speed to mix, then increase speed to medium and beat 30 seconds or until well combined and fluffy. Add brown sugar and granulated sugar and mix on low speed until well combined, about 20 seconds.

2 Add egg and vanilla and mix on low speed 10 seconds, then increase speed to medium and beat until well combined, about 30 seconds.

3 In a separate medium bowl, sift together flour, baking soda, and salt. Add dry ingredients to wet ingredients and mix on low speed until combined, about 20 seconds.

4 Cover dough and refrigerate 2 hours or overnight.

5 Preheat oven to 350°F and line a half sheet pan with parchment. Scoop dough into eight balls. Place four balls on prepared sheet pan and flatten with tines of a fork to form a crosshatch pattern on cookie.

6 Bake 12–15 minutes until cookies are set in center and lightly puffed. Cool 10 minutes on pan before transferring to a wire rack to cool completely. Repeat with remaining dough balls. Serve warm or at room temperature.

Domino's Chocolate Lava Crunch Cakes

Lava cakes were added to the Domino's menu in 2009 and quickly became a favorite with their crunchy crust and gooey filling. To keep the filling gooey, be sure to keep an eye on the cakes at the 20-minute mark so they do not overbake.

SERVES 2

1 tablespoon chocolate cookie crumbs, such as Oreo

4 ounces dark chocolate, chopped

4 ounces unsalted butter, room temperature

2 large eggs, room temperature

¼ cup granulated sugar

½ teaspoon pure vanilla extract

2 tablespoons plus 2 teaspoons all-purpose flour

2 teaspoons confectioners' sugar

1 Preheat oven to 350°F. Spray two 8-ounce ramekins with nonstick cooking spray. Divide cookie crumbs evenly between ramekins and shake each ramekin gently to evenly coat with crumbs.

2 In a medium microwave-safe bowl, add chocolate and butter. Heat on high 30 seconds, then stir. Continue to heat at 15-second intervals, stirring well between each interval, until melted.

3 In a separate medium bowl, add eggs and granulated sugar. Beat with a hand mixer on medium speed until light and fluffy, about 1 minute. Stir in vanilla and chocolate mixture and mix on low speed until well combined, then add flour and mix until smooth, about 15 seconds.

4 Divide batter evenly between ramekins. Bake 20–25 minutes until edges of each cake are firm and just starting to release from edges of ramekin but center of cake is still soft when gently pressed.

5 Cool cakes in ramekins 1 minute before running a thin knife around edges of ramekins and carefully turning cakes out onto serving plates. Serve immediately with a dusting of confectioners' sugar.

Domino's Cinna Stix

SERVES 6
(YIELDS 12 STICKS)

Pizza dough isn't just for pizza. This sweet recipe was created by Domino's employees looking for a quick snack using the ingredients they had on hand. This recipe will be especially appreciated by the kids in the family.

1 (16-ounce) package refrigerated pizza dough

¼ cup melted margarine

½ cup granulated sugar

2 teaspoons ground cinnamon

1 pound confectioners' sugar

1 tablespoon whole milk

1 tablespoon unsalted butter, melted

¼ teaspoon pure vanilla extract

1 Preheat oven to 350°F and lightly spray a half sheet pan with nonstick cooking spray.

2 Roll out pizza dough to a large rectangle. Brush melted margarine over dough.

3 In a small bowl, mix granulated sugar and cinnamon. Sprinkle mixture liberally over pizza dough. Cut dough in half and then slice into small sticks. Place dough on prepared baking sheet and bake 15 minutes.

4 In a separate small bowl, mix together confectioners' sugar, milk, butter, and vanilla. Serve alongside warm "stix" for dipping.

Golden Corral Bread Pudding

Golden Corral takes pride in the fact that they bake their desserts fresh each day. This recipe is a great way to use leftover rolls from the day before or bread that has lost its freshness.

SERVES 4–6

Pudding

2 cups whole milk

½ cup unsalted butter

2 large eggs

⅓ cup packed light brown sugar

¼ teaspoon salt

1 teaspoon ground cinnamon

3 cups cubed French bread

Sauce

1 cup whole milk

2 tablespoons unsalted butter

½ cup granulated sugar

1 teaspoon pure vanilla extract

1 tablespoon all-purpose flour

⅛ teaspoon salt

1 For the pudding: Preheat oven to 350°F and spray an 8" × 11" baking pan with nonstick cooking spray.

2 In a 1-quart saucepan over medium heat, heat milk and butter. Remove from heat and set aside. Let cool 30 minutes.

3 In a large bowl, beat eggs and add brown sugar, salt, and cinnamon. Add cooled milk mixture to egg mixture, making sure egg mixture does not curdle.

4 Add bread cubes and stir carefully to keep bread cubes from breaking apart.

5 Place bread mixture in prepared pan and bake 40 minutes or until a toothpick inserted into middle comes out clean. Set aside.

6 For the sauce: In a small saucepan, mix all ingredients together and bring to a boil 3–4 minutes, stirring constantly. Pour about half of sauce on warm pudding and place remainder in a serving bowl for those who desire a little extra. Serve immediately.

Mrs. Fields Chocolate Chip Cookies

**SERVES 15
(YIELDS 30 COOKIES)**

MRS. FIELDS

Mrs. Fields was founded in the late 1970s by a woman named Debbi Fields. She and her husband opened a store in California selling homemade cookies, which has grown into over 300 franchises around the world.

This popular mall cookie started from scratch in the home kitchen of founder Debbi Fields and spread across the nation. You can create it at home with simple ingredients.

1 cup unsalted butter, room temperature

½ cup granulated sugar

1½ cups packed light brown sugar

2 large eggs

2½ teaspoons pure vanilla extract

2½ cups all-purpose flour

¾ teaspoon salt

1 teaspoon baking powder

1 teaspoon baking soda

½ (18-ounce) bag semisweet chocolate chips

1 Preheat oven to 350°F and line a half sheet pan with parchment.

2 In a large bowl, cream together butter, sugars, eggs, and vanilla.

3 In a medium bowl, mix together flour, salt, baking powder, and baking soda.

4 Combine wet and dry ingredients until dry ingredients are just combined. Stir in chocolate chips.

5 Form golf ball–sized dough portions and place 2 inches apart on prepared baking sheet.

6 Bake 9–10 minutes until edges are lightly browned. Cool on pan 10 minutes, then transfer to a wire rack to cool completely. Serve at room temperature.

MRS. FIELDS CHOCOLATE CHIP COOKIES

Papa Johns Applepie

SERVES 8

DESSERT PIZZAS

Dessert pizzas have become a very hot item on many restaurant menus. They come in many varieties depending on the season and the local flavor. You can make your own crust from scratch of course, but this recipe calls for a ready-made store-bought crust found at any grocery store.

Dessert pizzas are typically made from pizza dough topped with a sweet filling, a crumble topping, and a glaze—and Papa Johns Applepie is no different. This version combines the best of pizza and apple pie for a sweet treat.

Pizza

1 (13.8-ounce) can refrigerated pizza dough

2 teaspoons vegetable oil

1 (21-ounce) can apple pie filling

½ cup all-purpose flour

½ cup packed light brown sugar

½ cup quick oats

½ cup cold unsalted butter

1 teaspoon ground cinnamon

Glaze

2 cups confectioners' sugar

3 tablespoons whole milk

1 tablespoon unsalted butter, melted

1 teaspoon pure vanilla extract

1 For the pizza: Preheat oven to 400°F.
2 Roll dough out on a floured surface to fit diameter of your pizza pan. Place dough on ungreased pan and form to edge of pan.
3 Brush dough with oil and prick with a fork. Prebake dough 3 minutes. Remove from oven.
4 Spread apple pie filling evenly over dough.
5 In a medium bowl, combine flour, brown sugar, oats, butter, and cinnamon with a fork or pastry blender. Spoon mixture over apple pie filling.
6 Return pizza to oven and bake 10–15 minutes until crust is light golden brown. Remove from oven.
7 For the glaze: In a small bowl, combine all ingredients. Drizzle glaze over pizza. Serve.

Papa Johns Cinnamon Pull Aparts

Added to the Papa Johns menu in 2016, these bite-sized cinnamon rolls topped with cream cheese drizzle are the perfect way to end a meal, or they can be enjoyed as a snack or even as breakfast!

SERVES 6

Pull Aparts

½ cup granulated sugar

2 teaspoons ground cinnamon, divided

⅓ cup plus 3 tablespoons (cubed and chilled) unsalted butter, divided

2 (8-ounce) cans biscuits, cut into quarters

⅓ cup packed light brown sugar

⅓ cup all-purpose flour

Drizzle

2 ounces cream cheese, room temperature

1 tablespoon unsalted butter, room temperature

½ cup confectioners' sugar

¼ teaspoon pure vanilla extract

1 teaspoon whole milk

1 For the pull aparts: Preheat oven to 350°F and spray an 8" × 8" square baking dish with nonstick cooking spray.

2 In a small bowl, combine granulated sugar and 1 teaspoon cinnamon. Whisk to combine.

3 In a small microwave-safe bowl, add ⅓ cup butter. Melt on high heat 30 seconds.

4 Dip biscuit pieces in butter, then roll in cinnamon sugar. Place in prepared pan.

5 In a medium bowl, mix together brown sugar, flour, remaining cinnamon, and remaining butter. With your fingers, rub mixture together to form a crumble having the consistency of sand. Sprinkle evenly over biscuit pieces in pan.

6 Bake 25–28 minutes until biscuit pieces are puffed and topping is golden brown.

7 For the drizzle: While pull aparts bake, in a separate medium bowl add all ingredients and mix with a hand mixer on low speed until smooth. Mixture should have the texture of hot fudge.

8 Remove pull aparts from oven, let cool 10 minutes, then drizzle with prepared drizzle. Serve warm.

Starbucks Cinnamon Coffee Cake

SERVES 9

Starbucks has had Cinnamon Coffee Cake, in one form or another, on their menu for years. Nothing goes better with a cup of coffee!

Cake

¾ cup unsalted butter, room temperature

1¼ cups granulated sugar

3 large eggs, room temperature

1¼ cups sour cream

2 teaspoons pure vanilla extract

2¼ cups all-purpose flour

2 teaspoons baking powder

½ teaspoon baking soda

¼ teaspoon salt

Streusel

½ cup packed light brown sugar

⅔ cup all-purpose flour

2 teaspoons ground cinnamon

4 tablespoons unsalted butter, cubed and chilled

1 For the cake: Preheat oven to 325°F and spray an 8" × 8" square pan with nonstick cooking spray.

2 In work bowl of a stand mixer or in a large bowl with a hand mixer, add butter and sugar. Beat on medium speed 1 minute until light and fluffy. Add eggs 1 at a time, beating 30 seconds after each addition.

3 In a small bowl, combine sour cream and vanilla and stir well.

4 In a medium bowl, sift together flour, baking powder, baking soda, and salt.

5 Add a third of sour cream mixture to butter mixture and mix on low speed 10 seconds. Add half of flour mixture and mix on low speed 15 seconds. Repeat with remaining sour cream mixture and flour mixture, ending with sour cream mixture.

6 For the streusel: In a separate medium bowl, add all ingredients and mix with your fingers until mixture resembles damp sand.

7 Pour half of cake batter into prepared pan. Sprinkle with a third of streusel mixture, then spread remaining batter over top. Evenly spread remaining streusel over top.

8 Bake 60–70 minutes until center of cake springs back when gently pressed. Cool completely in pan before serving.

Starbucks Iced Lemon Loaf

This popular Iced Lemon Loaf is served in thick slices that are perfect to enjoy with coffee or tea.

SERVES 8

Cake

1 cup granulated sugar

1 tablespoon lemon zest

1¾ cups all-purpose flour

1 teaspoon baking powder

¼ teaspoon baking soda

¼ teaspoon salt

½ cup low-fat buttermilk

¼ cup vegetable oil

2 tablespoons lemon juice

3 large eggs, room temperature

1 teaspoon pure vanilla extract

Glaze

1 cup confectioners' sugar

1 tablespoon unsalted butter, melted

2 teaspoons lemon juice

1 tablespoon heavy cream

1 For the cake: Preheat oven to 350°F and spray a 9" × 5" loaf pan with nonstick cooking spray.

2 In a large bowl, add sugar and lemon zest. Rub mixture between your fingers until sugar is very fragrant and zest is incorporated. Add flour, baking powder, baking soda, and salt and whisk to combine.

3 In a medium bowl, combine buttermilk, oil, lemon juice, eggs, and vanilla. Whisk until smooth, then add to dry ingredients and mix with a spatula until just combined with no large lumps, about 15–20 strokes.

4 Pour batter into prepared pan and draw a butter knife down center of batter to help cake rise evenly. Bake 50–60 minutes until center of cake springs back when gently pressed and edges of cake have released from sides of pan. Cool cake in pan 10 minutes, then turn out onto a wire rack to cool completely.

5 For the glaze: Once cake has cooled, add all ingredients to a medium bowl and whisk until smooth. Spoon glaze over top of cake, allowing it to drip down sides. Let stand at room temperature 1 hour before serving.

STARBUCKS ICED LEMON LOAF

Subway White Chip Macadamia Nut Cookies

While most people think of Subway for sandwiches, their cookies have developed something of a cult following. These white chocolate macadamia cookies are among their most popular cookie offerings.

SERVES 12
(YIELDS 24 COOKIES)

½ cup unsalted butter

¾ cup granulated sugar

1 large egg, room temperature

1 teaspoon pure vanilla extract

1¼ cups all-purpose flour

½ teaspoon baking soda

½ teaspoon salt

8 ounces chopped white chocolate

1 (6.5-ounce) jar chopped macadamia nuts

1 Preheat oven to 375°F.

2 In work bowl of a stand mixer fitted with paddle attachment or in a large bowl with a hand mixer, add butter and sugar. Beat on low speed 1 minute, then add egg and vanilla and beat 30 seconds.

3 In a medium bowl, combine flour, baking soda, and salt. Add flour mixture to butter mixture. Beat on low speed 30 seconds to combine. Add chocolate and nuts and mix 10 seconds to combine.

4 Drop cookies by heaping teaspoonfuls onto an ungreased half baking sheet, about 2 inches apart. Bake 8–10 minutes until lightly browned around edges.

5 Remove from oven and cool on baking sheet 10 minutes before transferring to a wire rack to cool completely. Serve.

Wendy's Frosty

SERVES 2

A menu classic for more than fifty years, the Frosty is an iconic treat! This copycat version makes a cool and refreshing frozen dairy dessert you can enjoy without leaving home.

¾ cup whole milk

¼ cup Hershey's Cocoa powder

4 cups vanilla ice cream

1 Combine all ingredients in a blender.
2 Blend on medium speed until creamy and thick. Stir if necessary.
3 If too thin, freeze mixture in serving cups until thicker.

WENDY'S FROSTY

CHAPTER 11

Drinks

Chili's Presidente Margarita

SERVES 1

Chili's is well-known for their margaritas, having had them on the menu from day one, and the Presidente Margarita is quite possibly one of the best and most iconic margaritas of all time.

1¼ ounces Sauza Commemorativo Añejo Tequila
½ ounce Presidente brandy
½ ounce Cointreau
4 ounces sour mix
1 teaspoon lime juice

Mix all ingredients together and serve in a salt-rimmed margarita glass filled with ice.

Cinnabon MochaLatte Chill

SERVES 2

The MochaLatta Chill is a sweet treat made with coffee and chocolate. It is perfect when you need a pick-me-up.

1 cup strong brewed coffee, chilled 2 hours
1 cup half-and-half
½ cup chocolate syrup
½ cup whipped cream

Combine coffee, half-and-half, and chocolate syrup in a small pitcher and stir well. Pour over ice in two (16-ounce) glasses. Top with whipped cream. Serve.

Dairy Queen Mocha MooLatté

Dairy Queen has you covered if you can't decide if you want ice cream or coffee. With their popular Mocha MooLatté, you don't have to choose! It is a creamy blend of ice cream and coffee topped with whipped cream and chocolate.

SERVES 2

⅓ cup granulated sugar

1 cup strong coffee

3 cups ice

2 cups vanilla ice cream

¼ cup whole milk

½ cup whipped cream

2 tablespoons chocolate syrup

1 Dissolve sugar in coffee. Refrigerate 1 hour or until cold.

2 Combine chilled coffee, ice, ice cream, and milk in a blender. Purée until ice is crushed and drink is smooth, about 45 seconds.

3 Pour into two (16-ounce) glasses and top with whipped cream and chocolate syrup. Serve.

Dave & Buster's Strawberry Watermelon Margarita

SERVES 2

This unique margarita uses watermelon juice and strawberry-infused ice cubes to make a margarita that is easy to crave. With this copycat recipe, you can enjoy it anytime the craving strikes!

1 cup fresh strawberries, hulled

1 tablespoon granulated sugar

4 cup fresh watermelon cubes

2 ounces Sauza Hacienda Silver Tequila

1 ounce DeKuyper Triple Sec Liqueur

1 ounce sweet and sour mix

1 In a blender, purée strawberries and sugar until smooth. Pass mixture through a strainer, then pour into an ice cube tray. Freeze until solid, about 3 hours.

2 In same blender, purée watermelon 1 minute, then pass through a strainer into a small pitcher. Refrigerate until ready to use.

3 In a shaker, add tequila, triple sec, sweet and sour, and watermelon juice. Shake 20 seconds or until mixture is very cold. Strain into two highball glasses and add frozen strawberry cubes. Serve immediately.

Dunkin' Donuts Iced Coffee

Dunkin' Donuts sells about 2 billion cups of coffee each year, and iced coffee sells more than hot. This recipe is very easy to make, and the simple syrup can be replaced with flavored coffee syrup if you prefer.

SERVES 1

1 tablespoon simple syrup

⅔ cup cold coffee

⅔ cup whole milk

4 ice cubes

In a large glass, add simple syrup, coffee, and milk. Stir to mix well. Add ice cubes and serve immediately.

Jack in the Box Oreo Shake

Cookies-and-cream lovers are sure to swoon for this extra-thick ice-cold treat! You can add a minty twist to this shake by adding $1/4$ teaspoon peppermint extract and a few drops of green food coloring.

SERVES 2

3 cups vanilla ice cream

1 cup whole milk

8 Oreo cookies

1 In a blender, purée ice cream and milk until smooth, about 45 seconds.
2 Break Oreo cookies in half and add to blender. Pulse ten times or until cookies are mostly puréed but a few larger pieces remain. Stir with a spoon to help incorporate cookies.
3 Pour shakes into two (12-ounce) glasses. Serve immediately.

MCDONALD'S CARAMEL FRAPPÉ

McDonald's Caramel Frappé

The McDonald's McCafé menu got its start in Australia in 1993 and joined the American menu in 2009 as a way to compete with Starbucks and their popular Frappuccino coffee drinks.

SERVES 2

2 cups ice

½ cup whole milk

½ cup strong coffee

2 tablespoons granulated sugar

2 tablespoons caramel syrup, plus more for drizzling

⅓ cup whipped cream

1 In a blender, purée ice, milk, coffee, sugar, and 2 tablespoons caramel syrup until smooth, about 30–40 seconds.

2 Divide into two tall glasses. Top each with whipped cream and drizzle with caramel syrup.

McDonald's French Vanilla Iced Coffee

McDonald's answer to the latte, this popular coffee drink is made with sweet French vanilla syrup, strong brewed coffee, and light cream. This version makes an even creamier drink you don't need to leave home for.

SERVES 6

6 tablespoons ground coffee

6⅓ cups cold water

14 ounces sweetened condensed milk

2 tablespoons pure vanilla extract

1 Brew coffee and water in a coffee maker. Cool 30 minutes or until warm but not hot.

2 Combine brewed coffee and condensed milk in a large pitcher. Stir until coffee and condensed milk are thoroughly blended. Stir in vanilla. Refrigerate until coffee is chilled, about 2 hours.

3 Serve in glasses filled with ice.

Orange Julius

SERVES 1

ORANGE JULIUS

The Orange Julius grew out of a California orange juice stand in the late 1920s. The stand was run by a man named Julius Freed, and the creamy texture of the drink recipe was developed by Bill Hamlin, Freed's real estate broker, to make the acid in the orange juice less bothersome to the stomach.

In 1926, Julius Freed opened a fresh orange juice stand, and a few years later started selling the popular Orange Julius. Once available in malls, today you can find it at Dairy Queen and, with this copycat recipe, at home.

6 ounces frozen orange juice concentrate

1 cup whole milk

1 cup water

¼ cup granulated sugar

1 teaspoon pure vanilla extract

8 ice cubes

1 In a blender, purée all ingredients except ice cubes 1–2 minutes.

2 While puréeing, open lid and add ice cubes 1 at a time, blending until smooth. Serve immediately.

ORANGE JULIUS

Red Lobster Boston Iced Tea

SERVES 1

Red Lobster's signature iced tea is one of their most popular nonalcoholic beverages, and comes in three flavors: the classic cranberry along with the newer mango and raspberry flavors.

1 cup brewed black tea

1 cup sweetened cranberry juice

In a pitcher, mix tea and cranberry juice. Fill a tall glass to the top with ice. Pour tea over ice and serve.

Sonic Cherry Limeade

SERVES 1

Sonic is known for its burgers and refreshing line of drinks and slushes. The most popular of these is the Cherry Limeade, which can be made with fewer calories if you swap regular Sprite for Sprite Zero.

1 (12-ounce) can Sprite

Juice of 3 lime wedges

¼ cup cherry juice

1. Fill a 16-ounce glass two-thirds of the way with ice.
2. Pour Sprite over ice. Squeeze lime juice into drink and drop wedges in. Add cherry juice and stir gently to combine. Serve with a straw.

Starbucks Iced Brown Sugar Oatmilk Shaken Espresso

SERVES 1

Added to the Starbucks menu in 2022, the Iced Brown Sugar Oatmilk Shaken Espresso has quickly become a fan favorite. For a deeper brown sugar flavor, you can use dark brown sugar for the light brown sugar.

2 tablespoons packed light brown sugar

2 tablespoons water

1 cup ice cubes

2 shots espresso

½ cup oat milk

1 In a small saucepan over medium heat, add brown sugar and water. Heat until sugar dissolves and syrup is hot. Remove from heat and allow to cool 20 minutes.

2 Add ice cubes to a large glass jar with a lid or to a cocktail shaker. Pour espresso and syrup over ice. Shake to mix. Pour into a tall glass and pour oat milk over top. Serve immediately.

Starbucks Mocha Frappucino Blended Beverage

SERVES 4

The Frappuccino debuted on the Starbucks menu in 1995 but got its start in 1993 during a heat wave in Los Angeles. Quick-thinking baristas were blending coffee drinks with ice, and a classic was born.

6 cups double-strength brewed dark roast coffee, divided

⅔ cup unsweetened cocoa powder, plus more for dusting

2 cups nonfat milk

1 Fill ice cube trays with 3 cups brewed coffee and place in freezer.

2 In a medium bowl, combine remaining brewed coffee, ⅔ cup cocoa powder, and milk and stir well to dissolve. Cover and chill.

3 Transfer prepared ice cubes to a large resealable plastic bag and crush cubes.

4 Fill four glasses with crushed ice and divide coffee and cocoa mixture evenly among glasses. Dust top of each glass with cocoa powder. Serve.

STARBUCKS PINK DRINK

Starbucks Pink Drink

This make-at-home version of the popular Starbucks drink has all the flavor and fun of the original at a fraction of the cost. Feel free to add simple syrup or other liquid sweetener if you prefer a sweeter drink. If you can't find freeze-dried strawberries, swap with 1/3 cup sliced fresh strawberries.

SERVES 1

1/2 cup boiling water

1 bag Tazo Passion Tea

1 cup white grape juice

1/2 cup unsweetened full-fat coconut milk

1/4 cup freeze-dried strawberries

1 In a heatproof cup, add boiling water and tea bag. Let steep 5 minutes. Remove tea bag and let tea cool to room temperature, about 30 minutes.

2 Once tea has cooled, mix well with white grape juice and coconut milk. Stir in freeze-dried strawberries.

3 Fill a tall glass with ice. Pour in tea mixture. Stir well. Serve immediately.

Tommy Bahama Classic Mojito

SERVES 1

Tommy Bahama is known for their rum drinks, and this take on the classic mojito is among their most popular. Fresh mint and lime juice are key to this drink, so be sure to use both for the best flavor.

2 sprigs fresh mint, divided

1 teaspoon superfine sugar

½ ounce fresh lime juice

2 ounces Cruzan Citrus Rum

½ cup crushed ice

3 tablespoons club soda

1 In a cocktail shaker, add 1 mint sprig, sugar, and lime juice. With a muddler or the handle of a wood spoon, crush until mint is bruised and sugar is dissolved.

2 Add rum and ice. Close and shake 30 seconds.

3 Pour mixture into a tall glass. Add club soda and garnish with remaining mint sprig.

Tommy Bahama Cucumber Smash

SERVES 1

This cool and refreshing drink is perfect for a hot summer day. Hendrick's Gin is infused with rose and cucumber, so it is a great choice for this beverage.

1-inch piece English cucumber, quartered

½ ounce fresh lime juice

1½ ounces Hendrick's Gin

¾ ounce elderflower liqueur

½ ounce simple syrup

½ cup crushed ice

1 ounce club soda

2 thin slices English cucumber, for garnish

1 In a rocks glass, add quartered cucumber and lime juice. With a muddler, crush cucumber until it is crushed in small pieces. Add gin, liqueur, and simple syrup and stir to combine. Add ice and stir well to chill drink.

2 Top drink with club soda and garnish with cucumber slices. Serve.

TOMMY BAHAMA CUCUMBER SMASH

Tommy Bahama Pain Killer #2

SERVES 1

This classic cocktail, originally created by Pusser's Rum Ltd., is a popular addition to the Tommy Bahama cocktail menu and combines dark rum, fruit juice, and cream of coconut.

4 ounces pineapple juice

2 ounces Pusser's Rum Blue Label

1 ounce fresh orange juice

1 ounce Coco Lopez cream of coconut

⅛ teaspoon freshly grated nutmeg

1 Fill a hurricane glass to the top with ice.

2 Mix together all ingredients except nutmeg in glass. Dust top of glass with nutmeg. Serve immediately.

STANDARD US/METRIC
MEASUREMENT CONVERSIONS

VOLUME CONVERSIONS

US Volume Measure	Metric Equivalent
⅛ teaspoon	0.5 milliliter
¼ teaspoon	1 milliliter
½ teaspoon	2 milliliters
1 teaspoon	5 milliliters
½ tablespoon	7 milliliters
1 tablespoon (3 teaspoons)	15 milliliters
2 tablespoons (1 fluid ounce)	30 milliliters
¼ cup (4 tablespoons)	60 milliliters
⅓ cup	90 milliliters
½ cup (4 fluid ounces)	125 milliliters
⅔ cup	160 milliliters
¾ cup (6 fluid ounces)	180 milliliters
1 cup (16 tablespoons)	250 milliliters
1 pint (2 cups)	500 milliliters
1 quart (4 cups)	1 liter (about)

WEIGHT CONVERSIONS

US Weight Measure	Metric Equivalent
½ ounce	15 grams
1 ounce	30 grams
2 ounces	60 grams
3 ounces	85 grams
¼ pound (4 ounces)	115 grams
½ pound (8 ounces)	225 grams
¾ pound (12 ounces)	340 grams
1 pound (16 ounces)	454 grams

OVEN TEMPERATURE CONVERSIONS

Degrees Fahrenheit	Degrees Celsius
200 degrees F	95 degrees C
250 degrees F	120 degrees C
275 degrees F	135 degrees C
300 degrees F	150 degrees C
325 degrees F	160 degrees C
350 degrees F	180 degrees C
375 degrees F	190 degrees C
400 degrees F	205 degrees C
425 degrees F	220 degrees C
450 degrees F	230 degrees C

BAKING PAN SIZES

American	Metric
8 × 1½ inch round baking pan	20 × 4 cm cake tin
9 × 1½ inch round baking pan	23 × 3.5 cm cake tin
11 × 7 × 1½ inch baking pan	28 × 18 × 4 cm baking tin
13 × 9 × 2 inch baking pan	30 × 20 × 5 cm baking tin
2 quart rectangular baking dish	30 × 20 × 3 cm baking tin
15 × 10 × 2 inch baking pan	30 × 25 × 2 cm baking tin (Swiss roll tin)
9 inch pie plate	22 × 4 or 23 × 4 cm pie plate
7 or 8 inch springform pan	18 or 20 cm springform or loose bottom cake tin
9 × 5 × 3 inch loaf pan	23 × 13 × 7 cm or 2 lb narrow loaf or pate tin
1½ quart casserole	1.5 liter casserole
2 quart casserole	2 liter casserole

Appendix A
Healthier Substitutions and Conversions

Bacon	Canadian bacon, turkey bacon, smoked turkey, or lean prosciutto (Italian ham)
White bread	Whole-wheat bread
White bread crumbs	Rolled oats, whole-wheat panko crumbs, or crushed bran cereal
Butter, margarine, shortening, or oil to prevent sticking	Cooking spray or nonstick pans
Cream cheese	Fat-free or low-fat cream cheese or fat-free ricotta cheese
Cheese	Low-fat or fat-free cheese
Eggs	Two egg whites or ¼ cup egg substitute for each whole egg
White flour	Whole-wheat flour for half of the called-for all-purpose flour
Ground beef	Extra-lean or lean ground beef, chicken, or turkey breast
Iceberg lettuce	Arugula, chicory, collard greens, dandelion greens, kale, mustard greens, spinach, or watercress
Whole milk	Evaporated skim milk or reduced-fat or fat-free milk
Pasta	Whole-wheat pasta
White rice	Brown rice, wild rice, bulgur, or pearl barley
Salad dressing	Fat-free or reduced-calorie dressing or flavored vinegars
Salt	Herbs, spices, fruit juices, salt-free seasoning mixes, or herb blends
Sour cream	Fat-free or low-fat sour cream, plain fat-free or low-fat yogurt
Soy sauce	Sweet-and-sour sauce, hot mustard sauce, or low-sodium soy sauce
Syrup	Puréed fruit, such as applesauce, or low-calorie, sugar-free syrup

Appendix B
Recipes Listed by Restaurant

A

Applebee's Bourbon Street Steaks

Applebee's Double-Glazed Baby Back Ribs

Applebee's Fiesta Lime Chicken

Applebee's Garlic Mashed Potatoes

Applebee's Oriental Chicken Salad

Applebee's Spinach & Artichoke Dip

Arby's Apple Turnovers

Arby's Classic Roast Beef Sandwiches

Auntie Anne's Pretzels

B

Bob Evans Bread & Celery Dressing

Bob Evans Mushroom & Onion Chopped Steaks

Bob Evans Reese's Peanut Butter Pie

Bob Evans Sausage Gravy with Biscuits

Bob Evans Slow-Roasted Turkey

Buca di Beppo Chicken Limone

Buca di Beppo Chicken Marsala

Buca di Beppo Chicken Saltimbocca

Buca di Beppo Lasagna

Buca di Beppo Spicy Chicken Rigatoni

Buffalo Wild Wings Asian Zing Cauliflower Wings

Buffalo Wild Wings Beer-Battered Onion Rings

Buffalo Wild Wings Boneless Wings

Buffalo Wild Wings Cheddar Cheese Curds

Buffalo Wild Wings Traditional Wings

Burger King Chicken Fries

Burger King French Toast Sticks

Burger King Fully Loaded Croissan'wich

C

California Pizza Kitchen Dakota Smashed Pea + Barley Soup

California Pizza Kitchen Italian Chopped Salad

California Pizza Kitchen Thai Crunch Salad

California Pizza Kitchen The Original BBQ Chicken Pizza

Carl's Jr. Big Angus Famous Star

Carl's Jr. Single Western Bacon Cheeseburger

Carrabba's Fettuccine Weesie

Carrabba's Italian Grill Meatballs

Carrabba's Linguine Pescatore

Cheesecake Factory Bang-Bang Chicken and Shrimp

Cheesecake Factory Cajun Jambalaya Pasta

Cheesecake Factory Crispy Crab Bites

Cheesecake Factory Fresh Strawberry Cheesecake

Cheesecake Factory Pumpkin Cheesecake

Chick-fil-A Chicken Sandwiches

Chick-fil-A Cobb Salad

Chick-fil-A Grilled Chicken Club Sandwiches

Chick-fil-A Waffle Potato Fries

Chili's Boneless Wings

Chili's Cajun Pasta

Chili's Chicken Enchilada Soup

Chili's Margarita Grilled Chicken

Chili's Molten Chocolate Cakes

Chili's Presidente Margarita

Chili's Southwestern Eggrolls

Chili's Texas Cheese Fries

Chipotle Beef Barbacoa

Chipotle Carnitas

Chipotle Chicken

Chipotle Cilantro Lime Rice

Chipotle Guacamole

Chipotle Queso Blanco

Cinnabon Cinnamon Rolls

Cinnabon MochaLatte Chill

Cracker Barrel Carrots

Cracker Barrel Cornbread Dressing

Cracker Barrel Corn Muffins

Cracker Barrel Fried Apples

Cracker Barrel Green Beans

Cracker Barrel Grilled Chicken Tenders

Cracker Barrel Hashbrown Casserole

Cracker Barrel Mmmm Mac N' Cheese

Cracker Barrel Momma's French Toast

Crumbl Birthday Cake Cookies

Crumbl Classic Pink Sugar Cookies

Crumbl Milk Chocolate Chip Cookies

Crumbl Ultimate Peanut Butter Cookies

D

Dairy Queen Mocha MooLatté

Dave & Buster's Pretzel Dogs

Dave & Buster's Strawberry Watermelon Margarita

Denny's Country Fried Steaks and Country Gravy

Denny's Pancake Puppies

Denny's Santa Fe Skillet

Domino's Chocolate Lava Crunch Cakes

Domino's Cinna Stix

Dunkin' Donuts Iced Coffee

G

Golden Corral Bread Pudding

Golden Corral Seafood Salad

H

Hardee's Mushroom & Swiss

Hooters Original Style Wings

I

IHOP Chicken Fajita Omelette

IHOP Colorado Omelette

IHOP New York Cheesecake Pancakes

IHOP Original Buttermilk Pancakes

In-N-Out Burger Double-Double

J

Jack in the Box Oreo Shake

Jack in the Box Sourdough Jack

Jack in the Box Tacos

Jersey Mike's Club Sub

Jersey Mike's The Original Italian

K

KFC Cole Slaw

KFC Mashed Potatoes and Gravy

KFC Secret Recipe Fries

KFC Sweet Corn

L

LongHorn Steakhouse Crispy Brussels Sprouts

LongHorn Steakhouse Loaded Potato Soup

LongHorn Steakhouse Outlaw Ribeye

LongHorn Steakhouse Parmesan Crusted Chicken

LongHorn Steakhouse White Cheddar Stuffed Mushrooms

Long John Silver's Fish

Long John Silver's Fish Tacos

M

McDonald's Bacon, Egg & Cheese Biscuit

McDonald's Breakfast Burritos

McDonald's Caramel Frappé

McDonald's Filet-O-Fish

McDonald's French Vanilla Iced Coffee

Mrs. Fields Chocolate Chip Cookies

O

O'Charley's Black & Bleu Caesar

O'Charley's Loaded Potato Soup

Olive Garden Breadsticks

Olive Garden Chicken & Gnocchi Soup

Olive Garden Chicken Scampi

Olive Garden House Salad

Olive Garden Pasta e Fagioli Soup

Olive Garden Toasted Ravioli

Olive Garden Zuppa Toscana

Orange Julius

Outback Steakhouse Aussie Cheese Fries

Outback Steakhouse Bloomin' Onion

Outback Steakhouse Gold Coast Coconut Shrimp

Outback Steakhouse Grilled Shrimp on the Barbie

Outback Steakhouse Sweet Potato

P

Panda Express Beijing Beef

Panda Express Chow Mein

Panda Express Fried Rice

Panda Express Honey Walnut Shrimp

Panda Express Orange Chicken

Panera Bread Broccoli Cheddar Soup

Panera Bread Chipotle Chicken Avocado Melt

Panera Bread Fuji Apple Salad with Chicken

Panera Bread Homestyle Chicken Noodle Soup

Panera Bread Mac & Cheese

Papa Johns Applepie

Papa Johns Cinnamon Pull Aparts

Papa Johns Garlic Knots

Papa Johns Italian Papadia

P.F. Chang's BBQ Pork Spare Ribs

P.F. Chang's Chicken Lettuce Wraps

P.F. Chang's Dynamite Shrimp

P.F. Chang's Mongolian Beef

P.F. Chang's Singapore Street Noodles

P.F. Chang's Stir-Fried Eggplant

P.F. Chang's Wonton Soup

Pizza Hut Original Stuffed Crust Pizza

Pizza Hut Oven-Baked Italian Meats Pasta

Popeyes Biscuits

Popeyes Chicken Sandwiches

Popeyes Red Beans & Rice

Popeyes Signature Chicken

Q

Quiznos French Dip

R

Red Lobster Boston Iced Tea

Red Lobster Cheddar Bay Biscuits

Red Lobster New England Clam Chowder

Red Lobster White Wine & Garlic Mussels

Red Robin Banzai

Red Robin Garlic Fries

Red Robin Royal Red Robin Burger

Red Robin Whiskey River BBQ

Ruby Tuesday New Orleans Seafood

S

Sonic Cherry Limeade

Sonic Fritos Chili Cheese Wraps

Sonic Hickory BBQ Cheeseburger

Starbucks Bacon & Gruyère Egg Bites

Starbucks Cinnamon Coffee Cake

Starbucks Iced Brown Sugar Oatmilk Shaken Espresso

Starbucks Iced Lemon Loaf

Starbucks Mocha Frappucino Blended Beverage

Starbucks Pink Drink

Subway Sweet Onion Chicken Teriyaki

Subway Tuna

Subway Veggie Delite Sandwich on Flatbread

Subway White Chip Macadamia Nut Cookies

T

Taco Bell Crunchwrap Supreme

Taco Bell Mexican Pizza

Texas Roadhouse Rolls with Honey Cinnamon Butter

TGI Fridays Loaded Potato Skins

TGI Fridays Sizzling Chicken & Cheese

TGI Fridays White Cheddar Broccoli Soup

Tommy Bahama Classic Mojito

Tommy Bahama Coconut Crusted Crab Cakes

Tommy Bahama Cucumber Smash

Tommy Bahama Lump Blue Crab Bisque

Tommy Bahama Pain Killer #2

W

Waffle House Biscuits & Gravy

Waffle House Cheesesteak Omelet

Waffle House Ham, Egg & Cheese
Hashbrown Bowl

Waffle House Hashbrowns

Waffle House Waffles

Wendy's Apple Pecan Salad

Wendy's Chili con Carne

Wendy's Frosty

Wendy's Spicy Chicken Sandwiches

White Castle Original Sliders

INDEX